# THE TRIANON ENIGMA
## My Friends Pictured Within

## by

## CHRIS GREEN

# ABOUT THE AUTHOR

Born in Ipswich, Emeritus Professor Chris Green OBE has had a long and distinguished career in education. He graduated from the University of Leeds with an honours degree in Psychology and Sociology before qualifying as a psychologist. He returned to the same University as a Research Fellow gaining a Doctorate in the psychology of music.

Teaching in primary schools, teacher training college and then higher education, led him into a professional career in the higher education sector eventually ending up as Regional Director for Anglia Polytechnic University and as Strategic Lead for Higher Education in the East of England.

His work in other fields, including mental health and the arts, together with broadcasting and print journalism eventually was recognised with the award of the Order of the British Empire in the New Year's Honours List 1994. He has been awarded Honorary Doctorates by the Universities of East Anglia and Essex. He has served on a number of national committees, whilst regionally he has been Chair of Ipswich Arts Association for many years.

He is married to Sylvia, with two sons, one an architect, the other an accountant and college business administrator.

"Family man, broadcaster, conductor & Professor".

# A WORD FROM CAMERON GREEN:

This is scary. Being published. I've only ever written before in school. Anyway, music. Let's not get off topic.

I play the bass guitar and, by the way if you don't know, I am Chris' grandson and live in Australia.

I am in Grade 6 – the last year of primary school – and am in the highest of the four bands at my school. Our band teacher, Penny, is wonderful and has been running the school's band programme for 20 years.

Because my Grandpa lives on the other side of the world (I hate planes), I don't get to see him in person much. I know he conducts the Trianon orchestra and choir and I have managed to go to a couple of his concerts.

When I auditioned for my school band, I put down drums, bass guitar and flute as instruments I would be happy playing. I would have ended up playing the flute but when I did the blow test (like the sorting hat in Harry Potter), my front teeth had just fallen out so I could not blow properly. Then they sent me to the trumpet but I just made rasping noises. So bass guitar it was, a nice easy-to-carry instrument (not) just like my parents asked for.

I hope to carry on playing music for a long time, and maybe play in Trianon if ever we are in the United Kingdom when there is a concert.

# ACKNOWLEDGEMENTS

When Moses (aka Charlton Heston) came down from the Mount with the Ten Commandments, I did not see a list of acknowledgements, but then Cecil B DeMille was its director and the reported 25,000 extras used in the film would require too much stone. I have no such problem because the list of extras is considerably shorter.

The seeds of the book were sown and liberally watered by Dominique Nightingale, Trianon's energetic Administrator. She has cajoled, threatened and encouraged me at times when the music had disappeared, but then as a Classical scholar who lectures frequently about the Greeks, she knew how to set me off on the right track.

Underpinning this writing has been the research undertaken by other Trianon members, notably Sally Marchant and Janet Dann, who have combed the copious archives we have, and supporting that, are the memories of Madeleine Rhodes and Ivan Gilson which have prompted new lines of enquiry.

One of the key archival documents that Trianon Music Committee members use is the directory of concert programmes and works performed compiled by Roger Hanes. Roger has been undertaking this work for years and the directory now runs into hundreds of pages. I have used it frequently in preparing the text of this book. Another team has been collating and choosing photographs. Much of the initial digitising has been undertaken by Ken Odam. The photos of Geoff Rogers are an important source in recent years. Other images were kindly and freely supplied by John Field (Ipswich buildings) and Alwyn Lewis (digital remastering of old photos).

The text may have started with me and I take full responsibility for any issues of commission or omission, but the editorial panel of Joy Bounds, Janet Dann, Diane Rich and especially Peter Willsher have been enormously valuable.

To the friends who have provided vignettes of their memories of Trianon, I am grateful. I would have liked to have included more, but I hope those we have featured give a broader view of what it felt like being members of this extraordinary group.

Finally to my family: to Sylvia, my wife; Julia, one of my sisters; and Jonathan, one of my sons, I would like to thank them for their support for much of my life in Trianon, and encouraging me to recall the many happy (and sad) memories that make the Group a living organism that has a musical soul.

**Chris Green**

# CONTENTS

# A FOREWORD FROM JOHN RUTTER CBE, PRESIDENT OF TRIANON

Dear Trianon Music Group,

As the old saying goes, if you want to change the world, start where you are, and for 60 years now Trianon Music Group has been changing the world for musicians and music-lovers in Suffolk and beyond. The range and scale of the group's achievement has been astounding and is surely a great cause for celebration.

So: mount a firework display, slice the birthday cake, open the champagne, but above all keep on making music for everyone's delight!

With my congratulations and good wishes,

John Rutter

*"John Rutter leading Trianon's 2013 singing workshop".*
*Photo credit Geoff Rogers*

# DIAMOND - A CELEBRATORY POEM FOR TRIANON MUSIC GROUP

## The Formation of Diamond

If, in the heat
of a world beginning,
you choose to share
that spark, your energy,

with others who – so
similar, so utterly distinct –
themselves reach, not only
back towards you but

out through space to,
say, three more who,
as they draw closer,
bring with them another

three – *et cetera* – all
holding and being held
in steadying, equal bonds:
this net, cast across

three dimensions, will, in
time (the fourth), catch
light, flash fire, write
*Love*, even on granite.


*Joanna Clark Vivian*

# CONGRATULATIONS TO PROF CHRIS GREEN AND TRIANON MUSIC GROUP ON SIXTY YEARS OF MUSIC-MAKING.

Wondering how to celebrate this Diamond Anniversary of Trianon Music Group – its founders, its members and all its achievements through the years – I thought: physical chemistry. Diamond is formed from pure carbon in the heat and high pressure of the earth's mantle. As the carbon atoms cool, or are compressed, they come close enough to one another to begin to form bonds: to share each other's energy. Each bond is a little bit like a taut rope, the invisible 'rope' being made up of energetic electrons – one from each atom – zipping about in the space between two carbon nuclei. In diamond, every carbon atom is joined in a giant net-like solid to four other carbons via such bonds, which are of equal strength throughout. This is what makes diamond so resilient – allowing it to be worked into gems whose facets reflect, transmit and refract light – resilient enough to make its mark, sometimes movingly, on the hardest rock.

Thank you, Chris, for asking me to write for Trianon.

*Dr. Joanna Clark Vivian, April 2019*

# OVERTURE

I have just been reading an article entitled *European History, 1950-2017* by historian Ian Kershaw in which he starts:

> *When I embarked on my most recent book, Roller-Coaster. Europe, 1950 - 2017, I remarked to a friend that I had a particularly daunting task ahead of me. He, however, was dismissive. 'It will be easy', he said. 'You will remember a lot of it.' At first sight, my friend seemed to have a point. After all, the decades since the Second World War largely coincide with my own lifetime (Kershaw was born a year after I was born), so I lived through all of what I was surveying and analysing in the book. How difficult could that be? Very difficult, as it turns out... (my book) has proved to be the most challenging book I've ever attempted"*
>
> *(BBC History Magazine, Oct. 2018).*

Now I cannot own up to being a prolific author, but I have written many theses and reports over the years and hundreds of articles, and I know exactly where Kershaw was coming from, because this has been my experience with this book.

But here goes... and like any good musical or opera, there has to be a short overture with some of the tunes that you will hear from time to time introduced.

This book is part personal recollection, with more than a touch of social history contained within, and that is where I start. Somewhere in this galaxy, light years ago, I sat with my two young sons watching a brand new movie called *Star Wars*. It was 1977, and actually the galaxy was not all that glamorous - it was the auditorium of the Gaumont Cinema, Ipswich (now the Ipswich Regent). Little did we realise that *Star Wars* would be followed by two sequels. Back then, that is where we thought the story ended.

A few years later the first "prequel" (itself a relatively newly invented word from the world of entertainment) appeared, and so we got Episode One. Now this made matters really confusing because the original *Star Wars* is renumbered as "Four", followed by two more prequels explaining how Episode Four and its characters came to be who they are, and why they are behaving the way they do.

You see, even in fantasy-land, things can get very confusing and it does not require George Lucas or composer/lyricist Stephen Sondheim to remind us of that. So, when it comes to explaining the trek that has taken me 60 years to achieve with Trianon, this actually needs a "prequel" and that is what you are going to get in Chapter One as I welcome you to *The Trianon Enigma- My Friends Pictured Within*.

Of course, like any good academic I should try to be original, but I have to confess at the outset that one of my favourite composers- Elgar- gave me the clue to suggesting a title. We had just performed his *Enigma Variations* which are, by coincidence, musical portraits of his friends pictured within the work. It has often been said that Trianon is like a large family, so the number of friends far exceeds the space that I have. Forgive me if hundreds have not been named, for you are there in my thoughts. However, what about that word "enigma", defined in the Oxford English Reference Dictionary as "puzzling thing or person" or "riddle or paradox"? The "puzzle" for me is how a small band of musicians – most at school or college (and therefore soon to be dispersed on various careers) with a time limit of their activity - would continue well past that expiry date and grow. "Paradox" in the sense that it should not have happened, but it did.

So, philological lesson over, let me take you back to the comfort of the 1950s. There had been a new Queen, Everest had been "conquered" and there was a disastrous mission to take the Suez Canal.

# CHAPTER ONE

# THE PREQUEL

***Where after sixty years of speculation the true genesis of the name Trianon is finally revealed.***

My, how things have changed since the first stirrings of Trianon, round about 1956. I had passed the 11+, sitting the test papers in what seemed like the overwhelming precincts of the Ipswich Borough Education Department in Tower Street, Ipswich (now the St Mary-le-Tower) and, like many other ten-year-olds, had found my way to the local grammar school - in my case, Northgate Grammar School for Boys. The other half of the population selected by this test were directed to the Northgate Grammar School for Girls, separated by a fence which, in my seven years there, gradually was being demolished by covert actions - mainly from the male side of the playing fields.

I have to confess that I was moderately talented then musically - I had been having piano and theory lessons with my godmother since I was about four, with violin added when I entered Northgate followed by organ and singing lessons. I even managed to achieved Grade VIII in four of these with the notable exception of the organ where mind, hands and feet never really worked in co-ordination.

At primary school, we would often join in music sessions courtesy of the British Broadcasting Corporation, who would transmit singing and music with movement sessions during class times. I had an enthusiastic music teacher who would rehearse the class in songs and class singing, with occasional comments about the excitement of going to concerts - we never did, but she did come in one day and breathlessly tell us about a new experience of going to Aldeburgh and a "new Festival" that had started there with "a Mr Pears singing accompanied by his friend, Mr Britten". Little did I think that I would meet them both in subsequent years and interview Peter Pears for a radio programme.

Anyway, I digress. When I got to secondary school, it was natural that I should soon get signed up for the embryo school orchestra but, unlike sports teams, there were fewer participants and so the orchestra was expanded to include musical girls from "next door" (that is the Girls' Grammar School). These included a pig-tailed young girl in ankle socks - Madeleine Haste - whom we now know as Maddy Rhodes, an Ipswich girl who played the violin and is still making music as a singer with Trianon and other choirs.

You see, even then, we needed that companionship, and the school orchestra was really born. We would be conducted by the new young music master, John Parry. I believe John had come to Northgate after a spell in the armed forces and reading music at Cambridge University. He provided a very different perspective to music study than that experienced by his colleagues.

I do not remember the Head of Music, Mr Graham, ever conducting us and despite that I had a great affection for him. I suspect that the lure of the Royal George pub, a brisk ten-minute walk from the school in Colchester Road, was more important (especially at lunchtime when rehearsals would take place), even though it did mean that, on one occasion, playing the school grand piano, he accompanied the end-of-autumn gathering in the Main Hall in a merry state. Rarely had O come all ye faithful sounded more like a "last orders please" rendition. Poor old but happy Harry!

Anyway, it was Harry who persuaded my mother that I should have violin lessons, and so enters the story one Miss Bertha Carter, a lady of great energy, determination and command of the sometimes rebellious musicians whom she taught individually or in classes. She worked for a splendid outfit called the Suffolk Rural Music School which had its base in Soane Street, Ipswich. Set up just after the Second World War in Hertfordshire, the Suffolk offshoot employed peripatetic teachers who would visit local primary and secondary schools teaching different instruments. Bertha was to play a significant role in the formation of Trianon, so remember her name.

One of the things that Bertha did was to organise "Playing days" - often held at Copleston School, Ipswich - when young musicians from various educational establishments would come together and "learn the classics". Often these sessions would be under the direction of an even more formidable lady, Elsie Smith. For a shy youngster such as myself, faced with a conductor who could shaft you with one glance, these experiences were frightening and yet intriguing. We often wondered whether our conductor engaged in one-arm wrestling? The other unintended consequence of this was to mix children from the grammar and secondary schools – a good thing when Britain was at the height it seems of a class divide.

So we were gradually introduced to music with intriguing titles like My love is an arbutus - it took me years to work out what that meant. I still cannot work out how "my love" would be like an "evergreen ericaceous tree or shrub". I also thought at the time that the word was like "arquebus" (an early type of portable gun). There would be a fair sparkling of marches like Handel's March from *Scipio (aka See the conquering hero comes)* and for light relief performances of Haydn's *Toy Symphony* - complete with cuckoo, quail, rattle and so on. It was considered very amusing especially when the cuckoo call was inadvertently inverted – if you see what I mean?

Musical gatherings like this were important adventures for many of us at a time when not many homes had televisions or cars, and the long-playing record had only begun to replace the black shellac discs with wind-up gramophones. It was also a time when some adults would still enjoy "musical evenings" whereby they would meet at someone's house and perform their "party pieces". Favourites I can remember were *I'll walk beside you, Little Boy Blue* and so on. It was only a short time before Bill Haley and the Comets would enter the musical vernacular and yet there was innocence about the social events.

In this motley collection of youngsters were my two closest friends - John Hart (who lived in the next road) and Lawrence Pizzey (who lived in another part of town). Both were contemporaries at Northgate Grammar School for Boys, and together we would engage in a range of activities, joined occasionally by other friends including Helen MacCrae, who lived in the next street close to John's house.

The activities included making some wholesome home movies facilitated by a present to me, a Eumig 8mm cine camera. We would devise scripts and films scenes (all silent because there was no sound track), and splice them together. One involved a visit to an empty dentist's surgery where we filmed a scene - think of the Health and Safety implications now. On another occasion we managed to negotiate a climb up the gasometer which bordered the Ipswich docks and filmed from the top there. I think I remained on the ground, directing the action, but I did co-write the script which is still in the archive. Of course, this may have burnished our reputation as budding film-makers then, but did little for our later careers. John went on to become an engineer and lives in the USA whilst Lawrence entered the Church of England ministry and rose to become a Canon. As for me? Well, that follows later.

So far you have encountered the school orchestra, the playing days and concerts organised by the Suffolk Rural Music School and the small group of friends and acquaintances who engaged in making films, putting on plays and sketches and enjoying themselves. Another type of musical enterprise was represented by the Ipswich Youth Orchestra. Friday tea-times at Christchurch Girls' School in Bolton Lane, Ipswich was when young people would come together and rehearse a slightly more advanced repertoire with a lot more competitive spirit amongst its more experienced players.

The Orchestra would meet during term times and some of its members - including myself - thought that it might be a good idea to continue meeting during holiday times.

What a heady mix of musical experiences! I was also very lucky because one of my uncles sang in the Ipswich Choral Society. He would take me to their concerts, usually in the Ipswich Corn Exchange (the Ipswich Public Hall in Tavern Street had burnt down during my early years). The current Ipswich Corn Exchange was a remodelling of the original internal building. If we have complaints nowadays about certain aspects of the venue, these are nothing compared to the venue in the 1940s and 1950s which had an oft-overwhelming aroma of flowers and rotting vegetable greens arising from its use as a market place for the sale of vegetables, fruits, flowers and grain. On concert days, the venue would often have been used earlier in the week as the market but like memories, the smells lingered on.

The ladies of the choir would come in full evening gown with corsages and new hair-dos. The men would all wear evening dress suits. The conductor - again a significant figure in the local music scene - was Dr W.H. Swinburne (newly arrived as Head of Music at North Essex Technical College, now Colchester Institute). My job was to become quite important. My uncle was Chairman of the Ipswich Choral Society, and he had invested in a reel-to-reel tape recorder. I was located high up in the gods to record the concerts. However, he had forgotten to check that the tape-recorder would pick up signals from the VHF messages emanating from the bowels of the Ipswich Town Hall (next door) where Ipswich Borough Constabulary had their headquarters. Only later, on replaying Handel's *Messiah*, did we find messages between the Police switchboard staff and the squad cars and police call boxes (blue boxes which have been inherited by Dr Who for his Tardis) punctuating choruses such as *And who shall abide?* It was particularly fitting for a chorus like *And we like sheep have gone astray* to hear a police officer being directed to investigate a drunk down by the still-working Ipswich docks.

I had a small circle of friends outside of school who met frequently. Coffee bars were just becoming the rage, but I suspect, looking back, that my group of friends and members of the youth club were more high-minded, and engaged in hiring tennis courts in Christchurch and Chantry parks on some evenings, and we would regularly meet at my home on Saturday evenings and organise our own entertainment. One of the highlights would be to rent a 16mm projector and screen plus the appropriate sound equipment from Ipswich Borough Council's Youth Department (yes, they had one then), and, armed with some films, we would organise film shows. The films were a mix of free promotional films from conglomerates like Shell, British Transport and the Post Office, and the feature films were usually pre-war cartoons or westerns rented from a second-hand shop in Fore Street called Sneezums. You collected them on a Friday and returned them on a Monday. So I learnt how to become a projectionist.

*"Market at the Corn Exchange, 1969: 'The venue had an oft-overwhelming aroma of flowers and rotting vegetable green...on concert days the smells lingered on'." Digital copy courtesy of David Kindred.*

"*Bertha Carter and her pupils at Northgate School for Boys, 1956. Middle row: Bertha (standing, 2nd left), Colin Moss and Chris Green; Jill Folley (with recorder, 5th from the left). Front row: Maddy Rhodes (4th from left).*"

"*Northgate Youth Orchestra (1958). Chris Green (seated, centre-left) and Maddy Rhodes (seated centre-right).*"

Occasionally we would organise outings and so the "Trianon Youth Group" emerged. Quite when the name originated I cannot remember, but I know I suggested it. I had recently been with my pen friend to Versailles, and somehow the name "Trianon" which I had seen stuck because, with my limited knowledge of Latin (that is another story, believe me), I thought there were three of us at the helm of this group - John Hart, Lawrence Pizzey and myself - hence "Tri"; and though we had names, "Anon" was a favourite one for musical titles. Hence "Trianon" came into being. There was no committee meeting to take a vote, we just chose it!

We organised drama evenings, even renting out a church hall and putting on a show in the best traditions of British and Hollywood films. Parents, families and friends were dragooned into attending so there was an audience and they even paid to come and see us! To my knowledge, no one asked for their money back. We printed our own programmes on our own printing press, with some archive material in the Trianon collection to prove it.

So, it was only a short step from that rather inward-looking small group of teenagers, to the suggestion that we should have an instrumental group that would meet in holiday-time. I have no idea again as to who suggested it, but I know that I collected names. Persuading a few players from the Ipswich Youth Orchestra, we formed the Trianon Youth Orchestra in 1959 and made our first outing. If I recall, it was to provide music at one of our local churches – a new one just opened on Chantry Estate in Ipswich. I conducted the small band and even arranged the orchestral parts which, I admit, was a bold move for I had to learn that violas played in a different clef. It would not be long before the same instrumentalists would give their first concert.

—§—

# TRIPS DOWN MEMORY LANE WITH FRIENDS

**JOHN HART:** *Trianon Memories at the Diamond Jubilee*

*(One of the three original members of the group of young people that would become the Trianon Youth Club)*

I was a teenager when I joined my friends Christopher Green and Lawrence Pizzey at the start of Trianon in 1956 as a musical and performance group dedicated to entertain anyone we could persuade to be in the audience.

This was from 1953 when we all attended Northgate Grammar School in Ipswich from the age of eleven. This was at a time when television was scarce (in my household we did not own a television set). We instead listened to the radio, read books and collected gramophone records that were developing from ten-inch 78 rpm shellac breakable discs, to 45 rpm seven-inch vinyl plastic discs which would grow to become twelve-inch extended play 33 1/3 rpm disks.

As a result, we looked to entertain ourselves with friends. Our transportation was by bicycle. I lived in the next street to Christopher and we had known each other from the age of 8. Our method of reaching each other's homes was to shin over a brick wall into a passageway to get access, which was shorter and quicker than walking by the road footpath.

We developed our concert entertainment into skits, short plays, musical interludes, film, readings and recitals. We widened our performance range and our audience by linking with the girls who attended a local dance studio. I have lived in the United States for over forty years now and have remained in contact with Christopher and I came back to visit with you at your 50th anniversary. Since the early days of Trianon Christopher has widened and developed the group into a choral and orchestral powerhouse and I am pleased to celebrate the Diamond Jubilee of the Trianon Music Group with them and wish them well in their future productions.

--§--

**CANNON LAWRENCE PIZZEY:** *What can I remember of the origins of Trianon 60 years ago?*

*(The second of the three former members of the group of young people that would become the Trianon Youth group)*

I remember that Chris, John and I were in the same form at Northgate. Chris and John lived very near one another and early on a Saturday morning I would have a piano lesson in Cobbold Street and then join the others at Chris's home in Christchurch Street. Many of our contemporaries spent Saturday mornings playing football or going to the Saturday morning pictures or train-spotting on Ipswich Station, but we met and enjoyed one another's company. Chris had a small home printing press, and we would type-set cards, invitations and tickets for Saturday evening entertainments which we would plan and run in the front room of Chris's home. These might include a film or two (on a small home projector); listening to recorded music; a short talk about someone's particular experience(s); a quiz and, inevitably, some refreshments. The venue meant we were limited in the number who could attend on any single occasion, but each occasion was a gathering of friends.

The move to a larger venue was accompanied by a change of content for the evenings. Chris invited members of the Northgate Schools Orchestra to meet also (eventually with other musicians) as a separate ensemble to practice and then perform an evening concert. This development was again based on friendship groups…. and so, like Topsy, Trianon grew! My own musical development was to be in Tower and Handbell Ringing – but I followed Trianon's orchestral and choral growth with interest and was pleased to host a concert some years back in St. Gregory's, Sudbury when I was the Rector of that parish.

"Great oaks from little acorns grow" – the three of us planted an acorn sixty years ago.

—§—

## HELEN MACRAE: *Memories of the beginnings of Trianon*

*(A classmate of Lawrence Pizzey at primary school, a friend of John Hart and then Chris Green when youngsters)*

In 1945, my father Captain J MacRae was appointed Harbour Master at Ipswich docks. This necessitated a move for our family from Scotland to a house in Humber Doucy Lane, Ipswich which went with my father's job. At that time, I had one brother, John, but was joined by another little person three years later, my brother Gordon.

At the age of 5, I attended St John's Church of England School in Cauldwell Hall Road. My memories from this time are pretty acute. I well remember laying down on mats in the hall for a rest. I was happy at school and even now can name at least two thirds of my class mates. I also recall our dinner ladies, Mrs Sparks and Mrs Baldry - always nice to them as it meant "second helpings".

An abiding memory is of our weekly spelling Bs which I always loved. We were lined up around the classroom and asked to spell various words. If you got it wrong, you had to sit down. This particular day it got down to Lawrence Pizzey (a founding member of the Trianon Youth Club) and me. Asked to spell the word "quire/choir", I opted for the former and was told to sit down. Lawrence spelled "choir" and subsequently won. For 67 years I've felt totally miffed, but somewhat placated to discover he became a vicar and is therefore one step away from God nowadays.

In 1952, my father went to work for the War Department in Cairn Ryan, on the west coast of Scotland. This, of course, meant we had to re-locate as our house went to the next Harbour Master. My mother decided in her wisdom that we would remain in Ipswich, whilst Dad left for Scotland. We moved to a house in Hervey Street. At the age of 11, I left St John's School to attend the Convent in Woodbridge Road, I think this was an attempt on my mother's part to turn me into a lady. Sadly this did not come to fruition. I joined the Guides at St Margaret's School each Friday night. I was in to the Thrush patrol (don't ask), and learnt knots, and how to peel back turf to make a fire. Skills I have never used since 1956. I did, however, make lots of friends, one of whom was Paula Shepherd who, I discovered only quite recently, married Garry Hart who lived down the road from me. He had a brother called John (the third founding member of the Trianon Youth Club), whom I always rather liked, but due to less-than-flattering short white ankle-socks and plaited hair which was an unattractive shade of mouse, complete with bows, didn't warrant a second glance.

I understand Garry subsequently became Lord Hart of Chilton – just down the road from where I now live, although he has now sadly passed away. I met up with Paula last year after many years of no contact and we had a wonderful get-together.

All the local youths joined St Margaret's Youth Club where we congregated, played table-tennis and had fun (Chris Green does not recall ever being a member). It was a great meeting place and regularly took precedence over maths homework. At the top of Hervey Street and Christchurch Street was a horse trough where we often gathered. Birkin Haward (subsequently a distinguished architect) and Trevor Nunn (the distinguished theatre director) were often to be seen with their bicycles. I often wonder what became of them?

I met Chris Green probably around the age of 13 or 14. He used to have piano lessons with Miss Doris Roe (his god mother) who lived at the bottom of Hervey Street as did I. We used to chat as he was leaving and I was going in for my lesson – also a vain attempt to shorten my time with Miss Roe to cover up the fact that I hadn't put in the required practice time. This is probably why Chris directs a music group now and I am really adept at playing Chopsticks.

Chris and I got on pretty well and I used to accompany him to a lot of his recitals. My mother was very impressed and for good measure made me sit in the front row – usually reserved for the vicar. Chris was obviously seriously into his music and destined for greater things. We knocked around for a few years until I started on the two-year NNEB course to fill in prior to commencing my SRN training at Anglesea Road Hospital.

Many years have now passed and I've lived in many places including three years in Africa. I returned to Suffolk when my husband retired, and sadly only had three years before he died.

I re-established contact with Chris when obtaining information from Ipswich Tourist Office which resulted in me attending one of his lectures about Films made in Suffolk. He gave an informative and humorous talk after which I went up to say "Hello". Luckily he remembered me. It is brilliant to see just how far he has travelled musically and very unexpected to meet up again. Old friends are the best. As for me, I still play a mean Chopstick.

—§—

## MADDY RHODES (NÉE HASTE): *The 1950s*

*(Violinist in Northgate School Orchestra, one of the first instrumentalists of Trianon Orchestra, then soprano in Trianon Choir which she still is to this day. She presides over many events, activities and tours as convener, general factotum and peace-maker.)*

Bertha Carter, my violin teacher, took her students to perform in churches on Sunday evenings. Once we went to The Round Church in Cambridge (I'm sure I haven't imagined that). It made a big impression, partly because I wore highish heels for the first time so it must have been 1958/59 and it was summertime.

She also arranged a visit to The Proms at the Royal Albert Hall. We went by coach from the 'Electric House' Ipswich and queued for the prom area. Peter & The Wolf was on the programme.

I have great memories too of the Music Weekends at Wolverstone Hall School involving music staff from Northgate Boys and Girls: John Parry, Head of Music at Northgate Boys' School, Gloria Firman, Head of Music at Northgate Girls' School (as she was before she became Gloria Wilson), Ipswich School Merlin Channon and Ipswich High School for Girls' Head of Music, Audrey Hill. What a beautiful setting and it was always sunny!! Did those weekends go on into the early 60s?

Social evenings included our version of *Top of the Pops* and *Juke Box Jury* (do you remember "I'll give it foive?"). I introduced *Vitava* by Smetana from *Ma Vlast* as my entry one evening.

—§—

# CHAPTER TWO

# THE SIXTIES

*During which the rag-tag bobtail collection of players becomes a small orchestra and gives its first public concerts. There is uncertainty about its future as its conductor goes off to University. Trianon acquires its first President whilst in the world at large there is the Cuban missile crisis and young people are able to enjoy newfound freedoms.*

It's odd. Somehow I cannot associate the word "Swinging" with "The Sixties". How did it pass me by - a youth in his prime, just on his way to University, and organising a group of young people making beautiful music? I suspect it is a fond memory created by the over-seventies to delude themselves that something really memorable was going on. Of course, Elvis was around and, before him, I recall hearing my first rock music when staying in France. I think it probably was Bill Haley and the Comets, and that was followed swiftly by "skiffle" and Lonnie Donegan.

Now you might think from that introduction, that the first decade of Trianon's existence was going to be a fairly boring affair. Perhaps it was, but at the time there were a lot of decisions to be made and challenges to be met. For a start, I had a year to think about what I was going to do as far as post-leaving school was concerned. It goes something like this. The assumption on most peoples' part was that I was going to read music at university. I had indeed achieved a pass at Scholarship level (a level beyond "A" Level), and even succeeded in getting an "O" Level pass in Latin - a necessary achievement if one wanted to enter Oxbridge at the time (GCE "O" levels were later replaced by GCSE). The success was even greater because it was despite a growing distrust and dislike on the part of the Latin teacher for my work and for me, to the point where he claimed that I had never done a decent day's work in my life!

But wait: my mother was a music teacher and from what I had experienced, it was a hard life making ends meet by teaching classes of pupils who really were not that interested, or waiting for pupils to turn up for their private lessons. I played the piano, organ (very poorly), violin and sang, achieving a high standard in all those things plus a few more on the way. Somehow, I could not see myself as an orchestral performer and the number of other opportunities seemed few and far between. Careers advice was minimal. The school I attended seemed far more interested in their pupils who aspired to enter Cambridge and Oxford Universities. One only had to enter the well-polished entrance hall to the Boys School to see the Honours Boards emblazoned with the names of former students who had graduated from those Universities. For those who had ventured beyond Oxbridge there was no mention, and this was at a time when the number of universities in Great Britain was a fraction of what it is today. (It is an irony that 40 years later I would be appointed by a government quango as one of nine people in England responsible for encouraging young people to enter higher education, and also creating a platform whereby thousands of them could study closer to home).

So, if not music, what to do? It was not uncommon then for students ending their school life to go into apprenticeships or into the world of commerce, but somehow the lure of going to university and a life away from Ipswich seemed attractive. What happened then I can reasonably blame on television. Our family had not long had a black and white television. One series that fascinated me was called *Probation Officer*. Why not become one of these? The only snag was that one had to be of a certain age to start specialist training. If I went immediately to university, I would have to wait a year before starting the next stage of training.

No-one at my school knew much about what the job entailed and certainly even less about the need to have a degree in social sciences. There were few books in the school library about Psychology, largely it seems because the Librarian thought that it was synonymous with Freud and that meant "sex". Therefore, pubescent young males should not be encouraged to have access to such tomes – this was a time when the Ipswich Borough Librarian had achieved fame through the national press when she banned Enid Blyton's Noddy from the public shelves.

Eventually someone discovered that a girl from the adjacent school had gone to a certain University to read social sciences (I had to discover that "reading" meant something specific in academic language), and I made contact with her. The resulting conversation during a holiday period made me about as informed as I would get. So, yours truly settled on Social Sciences and duly applied to various Universities, one of which summoned me for an interview.

The university was in Leeds. Imagine what it felt like to be disgorged from a steam train on to a grimy station platform at Leeds Central (no longer in existence) to find my way to lodgings for the night in this dark, sooty environment, when the only soot I had experienced in Ipswich was when the chimneys were swept. I and other applicants had explained to us what the" options" might be. Somehow the idea of combining Psychology and Sociology seemed interesting. A few weeks later, I received a letter confirming my place for September 1961 with chosen options as Economics and Philosophy.

What was the implication for Trianon? It meant that I was going be around in Ipswich for another year and my school had arranged to lease me out (or so it seemed) to the Ipswich Civic College where I could take some more "A" levels in seemingly relevant subjects which, in the end, turned out to be British Constitution, Economics and Public Affairs (and that really was not what I thought it would be. No mention of Mrs Simpson and the King). The experience was liberating - no need for a school uniform, mixing with people who had very interesting ideas, an anarchic tutor - all contributed to a year of exciting study. So, with more time on my hands and with a broadening social world, Trianon continued to meet and its activities extended.

I see from some of our archive that Trianon entered a team in the Ipswich Youth Quiz:

> In the finals of the Ipswich Youth Quiz, the Trianon team were narrowly beaten by Sidegate Lane Youth, by 29 points to 27 (March 16th). The team are to be congratulated on reaching the finals.

Looking through that same archive, it seems that the weeks were punctuated by informal music evenings and social events including a visit to see the ice-skating version of *Snow White and the Seven Dwarfs* at Wembley arena. This was followed by tea at Lyons Corner House, Piccadilly Circus, London with members arriving back in Ipswich at 11.45pm. (I did warn you that there was not much "swinging" in this decade).

I guess the most important event that starts the decade for Trianon is that the nascent orchestra makes it first concert appearance in January 1960 with a concert at Northgate Grammar School for Boys. It was cheap – as I recall the Head Teacher, Mr Norman Armstrong, loaned the room to us for the event. Although some of the orchestra had played together for other events prior to this, this is the launch of Trianon playing a medley of pieces borrowed from the Ipswich Borough Library, chosen by me and conducted by me as well – such was the state of our "democracy". In choosing that music, I had to have regard to what instruments were available - pretty much strings with some woodwind – and also that the string players could keep to first position. For those of you who are not string players, this has nothing to do with those books in the Boys' School library, but refers to the technical demands on string players. So "first position" equals the most rudimentary of finger positions and really is where we all began.

## Programme for 28th January 1960, Northgate Grammar School for Boys

| | |
|---|---|
| Rauzzini | Air in G |
| Haydn | Surprise Symphony (two movements) |
| Battishill | Air and Gavotte |
| Handel | Chaconne and Ritornello |
| Handel | Silent Worship |
| | Spring |
| Purcell | Air and Rondo in D minor |

It seems to have been the only concert that year, but it could not have been that bad because a year later we were back with another, extended, programme - again at Northgate, as listed and illustrated on the following two pages.

There was even a summer concert in June, when we extended our work by including pupils from the Ipswich High School conducted by their Director of Music, Audrey Hill. She had been an important figure in the occasional Music Days organised between the two Northgate Schools and the Ipswich High School (then situated in Westerfield Road, Ipswich).

By now it seems we were confident enough to charge admission, and the recorded prices were adults 1/6, children 9d. Another curious feature of this programme is that one of the composers seemed strangely familiar. I can assure you that Trianon's current Music Committee will never have to make the decision whether or not to perform something I have composed. The performers included soloists from within the orchestra including Peter Jennings who had become a mainstay of its organisation, Carol Long who would become a professional horn player in a number of national orchestras and David Lewis, our Leader at the time and who would serve as Best Man at my wedding.

# Programme for 28th January 1961, Northgate Grammar School

Conducted by Christopher Green

| | |
|---|---|
| Rauzzini | Air in G |
| Haydn | Minuet and Trio (Surprise Symphony) |
| Mozart | Clarinet Concerto K622 (Slow movement)<br>(Jeffrey Nancarrow clarinet, accompanied Beryl Howard) |
| Poulenc | Sonata piano duet<br>(Keith Ellis and Christopher Green) |
| Battishill | Air and Gavotte |
| Somervell | Shepherd's Cradle Song<br>(Beverley Coe, acc. Christopher Green) |
| Arne | When Daisies Pied  Items by a music group from Priory Heath Junior School accompanied by Mr N James |

---

| | |
|---|---|
| Haydn | Minuet and Presto |
| Handel | Chaconne and Ritornello |
| Boyce | Tell me lovely shepherd     (Beverley Coe) |
| Phillips | Sing Joyous Bird          (Beverley Coe) |
| | Violin solos by David Lewis, acc. Carol Long |
| | Piano solos by Keith Ellis |
| | Items by a music group from Priory Heath Junior School |
| Purcell | Air and Rondo in D Minor |

trianon
youth
club
Presents a

# CONCERT

with the

TRIANON YOUTH ORCHESTRA

conductor

Christopher Green

and

soloists

SATURDAY, 28th JANUARY   at 7.15 p.m. in the MUSIC ROOM AT THE
NORTHGATE GRAMMAR SCHOOL FOR BOYS
(by kind permission of the Head Master)

ADMISSION BY PROGRAMME

ADULTS 1/-
CHILDREN UNDER 14
9d.

## THE ORCHESTRA

**1st Violins**
Carol Long (Leader)
Eylene Doolen
R. James
Ann Trewby
Carol Jarrold
Beryl Howard
Miss A.B. Carter

**2nd Violins**
C. Moss
M. Gould
J. Allen
D. Halls
D. Lewis
A. Woods

**Viola**
D. Mildenhall

**Cellos**
J. Drake
P. Jennings

**Clarinets**
Carole Mitchell
G. Nancarrow
B. Cloke
C. Gibbens

**Flutes**
M. Martin
C. Mallett

-------------

NATIONAL --------- ANTHEM

| | | |
|---|---|---|
| Orchestra | Air in G | Rauzzini |
| | Minuet & Trio (Surprise Symphony) | Haydn |
| Solo | Slow movement Clarinet Concerto K622 | Mozart |
| | Jeffrey Nancarrow accompanied by Beryl Howard. | |
| Piano Duet | Sonata | Poulenc |
| | Keith Ellis & Christopher Green | |
| Orchestra | Air & Gavotte | Battishill |
| Vocal Solos | Shepherd's Cradle Song | Somervell |
| | When Daisies Pied | Arne |
| | Beverley Coe accompanied by Christopher Green | |
| Items by | A Music group from Priory Heath Junior School accompanied by Mr. N. James. | |

The Orchestra sponsored by Trianon Youth Club meet when the occasion arises.   It does much accompanying work for church services.   Its members are all still at school; many are taking up music as a career, but the orchestra is formed solely for enjoyment.

| | | |
|---|---|---|
| Orchestra | Minuet & Presto | Haydn |
| | Two movements Chaconne & Ritornello. | Handel |
| Vocal Solos | Tell me lovely shepherd | Boyce |
| | Sing Joyous Bird | Phillips |
| | Beverley Coe. | |
| Violin Solos | by David Lewis accompanied by Carol Long. | |
| Orchestra | Two song by Handel. | Silent Worship |
| | | Spring |
| Piano Solos | Keith Ellis | |
| Items by | A Music Group from Priory Heath | |
| Orchestra | Air & Rondo in D. Minor | Purcell |

We are indebted to Miss A.B. Carter for her help in the concert and for the loan of music;  to the soloists and to Mr. N.James for bringing the group from Priory Heath. Also to Mr. Colin Moss for acting as business manager.

*"Programme from the concert of 28th January 1961."*

# **Programme for 10th June 1961, Northgate Grammar School**

Conducted by Christopher Green

With soloists and a section of The Ipswich High School Choir, conducted by Audrey Hill.

| | |
|---|---|
| Handel | Two marches: 'Joshua' (arr. Christopher Green) and 'Scipio' (arr. Charles Woodhouse) |
| Debussy | Petite Suite (piano duet) (Peter Jennings, John Drake) |
| Mozart | Ave Verum |
| | Vocal solos performed by Celia Noon acc. Carol Long |
| Carse | Sea Suite (Robin James & Martin Goold, violins) |
| | Choir items |
| J. H.Roman | Suite |

---

| | | |
|---|---|---|
| Kuchler | Violin Concertino in D Major | (David Lewis) |
| Mozart | Vocal Solos | (Celia Noon) |
| Mozart | Andante | |
| Mozart | Slow movement from Quintet E flat Major (Jeffrey Nancarrow - clarinet, Keith Ellis – piano) | |
| Dohnanyi | Rhapsody No 4 in F sharp minor (Carol Long - piano) | |
| Haydn | Toy Symphony - from the Cassation in G | |
| | Choir items | |
| | C Green | Scenes: Woodland, Nautical and Ceremonial Scene |

There was even a preview of the event, published in the "Youth and Adult Activities" section of the *Ipswich Evening Star* in June of that year:

> *The Trianon Youth Orchestra conducted by Christopher Green is holding a concert on Saturday, June 10th at 7.15 p.m. at the Northgate Grammar School for Boys. The varied programme will include works by Handel, Haydn, and the first performance of 'Scenes' by Christopher Green which was written especially for the concert. There will also be soloists and a section of the Ipswich High school choir will be singing. Programmes can be obtained from 62, Christchurch Street, telephone number: 55784, or any member of the orchestra.     ORGANISER*

By September 1961 I was back in the grimy city of Leeds discovering what a large University would be like, and also the "hot" spots. As far as I was concerned it was less to do with the Students' Union and its bars, rather more to do with the Saturday night concerts in the Victorian edifice that was Leeds Town Hall. For a small sum one could enjoy orchestras that included the Warsaw Philharmonic, Czech Philharmonic, Hallé, and Royal Liverpool Philharmonic. Then it was the No 1 bus back to Lawnswood (a suburb of Leeds) and the new Hall of Residence which I was one of the first to enter.

Trianon concerts proceeded spasmodically with about 20-30 players during the undergraduate years with little expectation that we would continue once I had graduated – but that seemed a long way away. During those years we continued to perform at Northgate and then ventured to the Ipswich Art Gallery (adjacent to the Ipswich Museum). This is what the reviewer had to say about the concert in January which featured my singing teacher, Miss Olive Foster (who also taught many of my contemporaries), whilst one of the cello players - John Drake - joined me conducting when he directed a wind ensemble. John went on to become a musicologist in Durham and sadly one of the Trianon members who died at a young age. We also teamed up with a local school whose Head Teacher (and father of two of our members), Mr James, trained his pupils who played recorder and mouth organs – the only time a Trianon concert has featured those plaintive little instruments.

Monday January 7th: "An Ambitious Programme"

> *For their Christmas holiday concert the Trianon Youth Orchestra, made up of 70 per cent school children with some adults to help out, presented a varied, interesting and ambitious programme on Saturday night at the Art Gallery, Ipswich. Their conductor is Christopher Green, an undergraduate at Leeds University. He is also the director of the orchestra, trains the members and is responsible for the interpretation of the music. It is very rare to have someone so young to be in complete charge of an orchestra. What the orchestra lack in experience they make up for in keenness and willingness to*

*tackle anything. They played some little known pieces, and on the whole they were well handled, though the music could have been played more crisply in most of the works. The orchestra was strongest in the wind section, and Mozart's 'Minuet and Trio from Serenade in B flat' by the wind ensemble conducted by John Drake, the assistant conductor was well done. Their most ambitious work was the 'Symphony in C' by I.J.Pleyel, a little-known composer, and though perhaps sometimes it lacked cohesion it was a good attempt. Julian Mallett was the soloist in the Flute Concerto in D (known as 'The Goldfinch') by A. Vivaldi, and he handled the cadenzas imitating the bird's song competently and with a light touch. He was well backed by the orchestra. Mollie Southgate, accompanied by Miss O. Foster, gave some pleasing solos, though she was a little uncertain on her higher notes. Pupils from the Priory Heath Junior School, with their conductor, Mr. H. N. James, gave a number of pieces on recorders and mouth organs.*

It was one of those chance events that produced a memorable gain for Trianon. My mother had augmented the somewhat sparse earnings from music-teaching by taking on the job of part-time nursing auxiliary at the Ipswich and East Suffolk Hospital, Anglesea Road, Ipswich. One of her patients was Miss Imogen Holst and in conversation she mentioned to Imo (the name by which many of her friends and acquaintances would affectionately call her) that her son had set up this music group of young players. Imo, as was always the case, showed enthusiasm and probably said something like "Get Christopher (I was always Christopher to her) to contact me". I did and before long she telegraphed me to accept becoming the first President of Trianon. That was a major coup for us because she was highly regarded then as Benjamin Britten's assistant. It was later that her father's music began to figure largely in our repertoire and only more recently has Imogen's creativity as a composer become recognised.

*"Telegram from Imogen Holst to Chris Green"*

Imogen – with her great experience of working with amateur performers – became a front-line person to whom to turn for advice and, during her time as President, she came to conduct Trianon bringing with her some of her father's less well-known music. I would visit her flat in Aldeburgh to meet with her and, of course, the conversation was punctuated by references to the work she was currently undertaking for Benjamin Britten. The biographies of Imogen detail that so well, and make reference to Trianon:

> *The enterprising Trianon Music Group for young players and singers (aged thirteen to twenty-five) was based in Ipswich. She heard of the group during a stay in hospital, where one of her nurses was the mother of the Group's director, Christopher Green, and became its President in 1961. The (Trianon) Suite takes all sections of the orchestra into account, and the third movement has an important part for piano solo.*
>
> *(Imogen Holst – A Life in Music Aldeburgh Studies in Music, Boydell 2007)*

*"Imogen Holst, first President of Trianon." Photo credit: Alamy.*

The next break-through came later in 1963 when we felt confident enough to move from the intimate Ipswich Art Gallery to the main hall of the Ipswich Co-operative Society. Situated on the upper floor of the now forlorn Ipswich Co-operative Society building in Carr Street, this was a spacious hall – or so it seemed - and we certainly managed to get an audience, mostly families, for a slightly more ambitious programme –

## Programme for 20th July 1963, Summer Concert at Co-op Hall, Ipswich

| | |
|---|---|
| Cimarosa | Overture 'The Impresario' |
| Holst | Brook Green Suite |
| Handel | Concerto for Trumpet and Strings |
| Vaughan-Williams | English Folk Suite |
| Chabrier | Joyeuse Marche |
| Bizet | L'Arlesienne Suite |

Looking again at the contents of the programme, I realise that the membership must have grown from the more baroque or chamber ensemble we fielded in the previous and early concerts. That was underlined by the fact that within a few weeks we were back at the same hall and joined by the Ipswich Co-op Girls' Choir (celebrated at the time) and the buglers of the Ipswich Sea Cadet Corps.

January 1964 produced a new development – a larger venue: the School Hall at Christchurch Girls' School, Bolton Lane - an annex of Tower Ramparts Secondary Modern School (the main building being located on the site that is now occupied by Sailmakers). In that programme, a singing group made up of orchestra members makes its first appearance. This would, in time, develop into the Trianon Singers and then Trianon Choir. Its members were mostly members of the orchestra who could sing, plus a few extras to augment the male sections.

It looked like Trianon was here to stay, but there were question marks. Within a few months I would be sitting the finals examination for my degree - it was a Combined Honours in Psychology and Sociology taught by some lecturers who would shortly move to the newly created University of Essex and cause havoc there. I had also met a young student, Sylvia, who was studying Mathematics and Physics (so making good my very distinct incompetence at mathematics). What was I going to do?

One of the Lecturers in the Department of Music, James Brown, came from Ipswich and became a great friend over those years. He was a distinguished organist and would eventually play at the wedding between Sylvia and myself in 1968. James was also a composer and would write *A Miniature Symphony* for Trianon to perform.

James had already put me in contact with several musicians who were conductors in order for me to develop my conducting skills. Arthur Butterworth, a great name in the brass-banding world was one, as was George Hurst, then Principal Conductor of the BBC Northern Orchestra (now the BBC Philharmonic). Although nothing really positive came from that, one person whom he recommended and with whom I had close contact during the Leeds years was a singing teacher, Madame Stiles-Allen. In those days, one always addressed teachers of her gender and standing with the appellation, "Madame".

*"The Civic College, Ipswich, which provided an early concert venue, and in which Chris took some A-Levels."*

*"Muriel Green (pictured right), Chris's mother, who introduced Imogen Holst to Chris while she was nursing her at Ipswich Hospital."*

"Pictured from left: Dave Lewis (one of Trianon's leaders), Carole Long (the first leader), Chris Green, Janet Oldham and Rosemary Humphries née James."

"Choir performing at the Civic College in 1963. Front row from left: Pat Garnham, her sister Linda, and Janet Armitage. Second row, far right: Maddy Rhodes."

STILES-ALLEN

*Very Sincerely Yours [signature]*

I turned up at Madame Stiles-Allen's imposing residence in Headingley, a suburb of Leeds, to be met by an equally imposing lady who took me back to the basic principles of voice production. What I remembered were some pretty agonising physical sessions in sharp comparison to the somewhat relaxed lessons that I had enjoyed with a local teacher in Ipswich. Madame would regale me with stories about her former pupils which included a young Julie Andrews. I knew little about her, except that she made me do vocal exercises in a painful way. However, I found the cost of continued lessons to be impossible to maintain and they came to an end. What had I missed? Well, a lot. Only much later, did I discover from my father that she had been a distinguished solo artist, one of Sir Henry Wood's friends and one of the sixteen who were included in the first performance of Vaughan Williams' *Serenade to Music*. Her name is listed in the vocal score as testament to that event.

Back to James who suggested I develop my interest in music in another way. That was to register for a research degree combining Psychology and Music. Once again, there was a great scampering around because no one had ever done that at Leeds and it needed financing. First I had to prove to the Heads of the Psychology and Music Departments that I had the motivation and skills to register for a Doctor of Philosophy degree.

Ipswich Borough Council – in its final days as a unitary authority responsible for education – awarded me a grant, and so I began my second career as a Research Fellow back at Leeds developing a programme of research that would investigate the development of musical taste. Looking back, this was a field where few had ventured (I now know why), and it was long before the Psychology of Music became a well-known field of research. Living costs were supplemented by acting as a Demonstrator for Psychology laboratory classes, and as Tutor to first year students, including delightful groups of American students who spent the year at Leeds.

The bigger question kept arising: how to keep Trianon going? We had to source a rehearsal space and this is where my life as a young Boy Scout came in handy. I had belonged to the 17th Ipswich Scout group whose Scoutmaster was an energetic Roy Goody, who also produced the Ipswich Gang Shows. By the 1960s, the Ipswich Scouts Association had taken over the lease of a run-down set of halls in Arcade Street and so I used the connection to book the Library and Main Hall from the Association for rehearsals. With the help of some of our players and singers who remained in Ipswich, we managed to cobble together a rehearsal programme and Newsletter which were produced - illicitly, I confess – on the Roneo duplicator (a messy ink machine using a master copy typed on to a special layer) at the Department of Psychology at Leeds University and mailed out to members. Remember no photocopiers of any useful kind existed and social media had not even been thought of, for this was still the time of slide-rules.

One of the threads that should stand out through this history of Trianon is "Communication". The issue had already started with my period in Leeds with members strewn across Suffolk. In due course the geographical spread would reach well into Essex and South Norfolk. So the challenge came as to how to keep everyone informed of what was going on. Up to now, a small band of members had made sure people knew when rehearsals would take place. Their memories may still be good enough to recall the frantic calls that would be made through the means of long-distance BT trunk calls. It did not take much to come up with the idea of a Newsletter and in 1964, Trianon News was published for the first time. This informal and informed little magazine would wing its way to members three times each year and, I am happy to say, continues to this day.

Before we reach the end of the 1960s – those "Swinging" (?) times - we had moved around with our concerts, one in Dedham Parish Church in 1965 attended by a handful of people – mostly my family who lived in the village. We achieved greater things by moving to the Ipswich School where the choir really made itself felt with a programme that included Vaughan Williams' *In Windsor Forest*. Indeed, the Great School at the Ipswich School became our regular venue, aided and assisted by the Director of Music at the time, John Ince. John - a delightfully anarchic fellow – came to our rescue on more than occasion and "fixed" our venue and many other things for which I was grateful.

The January 1966 concert started with Cimarosa's Overture to *The Secret Marriage*, but my engagement to Sylvia and our wedding plans were more public and two years off. I was nearing the end of my research degree and in 1967, I was off again by train - to Edinburgh University where I was to sit the viva. Arriving early in the morning from a sleeper from King's Cross was not the best way to sit a three-hour grilling, and so I was subdued and dismayed to find that I had to do some more revision to my thesis before I would be awarded a Doctor of Philosophy degree.

Yet more decisions as 1967 came to an end and I had to find a job. Once again, perhaps someone else could take over conducting Trianon? I was, after all, being helped by various members including John Ince and a very young Russell Hawes, a member of the choir and a pupil at Northgate Boys' School, about to go off to Music Conservatoire.

Somehow things fell into place with my appointment as an Assistant Lecturer (the lowest of the low) at an all- female Teacher Training College in Hertfordshire. It was commutable to Ipswich and so we kept rehearsing. One of the conditions of my appointment was to get teaching experience in primary schools, and so it was that I entered three primary schools in Ipswich for a spell starting at Whitton, then Ranelagh Road School and ending up at the newly opened Dale Hall School. Perfect really, because I was being paid a wage, I was in Ipswich and Trianon would continue for a while.

My fiancée Sylvia had just graduated and was undertaking her Postgraduate Certificate in Education in Leeds. That completed she was appointed as a Mathematics Teacher at Leeds Girls' High School. The appointment was short-lived because by August 1968 we got married and settled in Braintree, Essex. At that time, it was midway between Bishops Stortford and Ipswich. Little did I know that I would be ploughing that route for another 50 plus years. Whilst I was teaching in the town at the aforementioned College (run by a fearsome Principal whose verbal abuse of young male teaching staff was becoming apparent), Sylvia obtained post as a teacher of maths, physics and sports at the local High School. Everything seemed fine - or was it?

Trianon was working well, and by 1969 we had moved to St John's Church, Cauldwell Hall Road, Ipswich for concerts with conducting sometimes shared with other members of Trianon. We even had a Management Committee by now with a Chairman. In fact, we had had a Chairman along with Secretaries and Treasurers since the beginning. The post of first Chairman was occupied by Dr Roy Coates. Roy, who lived with his wife in Felixstowe, played the trombone and composed various pieces of music. He remained Chairman until his untimely death in 1970.

To continue the story, we needed the security of rehearsal space and a venue. By the end of the 1960s, the orchestral repertoire had extended to include symphonies from the Romantic period and works by contemporary composers including Malcolm Arnold (again a name and person with whom I would become acquainted in the 1970s). We were served by an excellent leader, a member of Trianon's first violin section and a local student, Howard Griffiths. I am delighted to come across his name from time to time as conductor of many CD recordings by Swiss and German orchestras, and he has been Principal Conductor of the Brandenburg State Orchestra of Frankfurt.

There was one other development that had happened in the 1960s. Through the Ipswich Education Office Trianon was approached to see if we would be interested in partnering a Youth Orchestra that would be visiting from a town called Detmold in West Germany, So it was that we encountered some lifelong friends who accompanied the party of young musicians – Herr Harry Asef and his assistant, Hildegard. I think the party came twice, but I recall their first visit was not the best organised starting with their decision to stay in a newly created motel at Felixstowe Docks - really designed for lorry drivers. Still, we had some fun including a memorable visit to Ely Cathedral. Cut to a coachload of youngsters and their back-up team journeying across East Anglia to see the cathedral, arriving 10 minutes before the doors were shut (we had not checked whether the Cathedral would be open all day on a Sunday) and then finding that the town was closed - so having to improvise a journey back to Ipswich trying to maintain interest amongst said youngsters. The cricket match being played at Cavendish, Suffolk did little to engage them. What puzzled me for days afterwards is why was Ely chosen by the Germans?

The answer was simple. Their conductor, Herr Gresser, a formidable gentleman of large proportions, had decided that was where they would visit! But why? On the confidential side of things, Harry Asef (the party's interpreter) explained to me that the conductor had been in the Luftwaffe during the Second World War and they had used the Cathedral tower at Ely as a navigational aid when they were going to bomb the Midlands. He wanted to see the place from the ground.

So as the 1960s comes to an end - and I have somehow missed out on that "Swingin' feeling" - what's been achieved? Well, Trianon has bedded itself in with an expanding repertoire and a growing audience. We have acquired our first President. The Choir has been formed and we have ventured to new venues to perform. We have encountered our first European music group, which lead us in the last months of the sixties into planning a return visit to West Germany (remember, Germany was still portioned into East and West) in 1970. This will be the first time Trianon will have performed on mainland Europe and what a visit! Were they ready for us? Read on and find out.

# TRIPS DOWN MEMORY LANE WITH FRIENDS

**JULIA GREEN:** *Pretending to be the Trianon Postie*

*(Chris's youngest sister)*

It's time for rehearsals to begin and I am the first to go back ready as the timps and boxes of stands have to be moved to the Ipswich Scouts Headquarters in Arcade Street in a hire van. Who should be at the helm but my brother, Chris, and Peter Willsher (Trianon timpanist at the time)? I was six years old and idolised my big brother (and still do now after more than 50 years). So, wherever he went he would have his little sister whether he liked it or not - poor thing.

The hire van would be collected by us and I had the sheer fun of sitting and standing in the back before and after the instruments had been collected.

The rehearsals took place mainly at the Scouts HQ. I would carry my brother's music bag, no matter how full of music it may have been. There was not a lift at the Scouts HQ so we would climb up six flights of stone stairs. The hall was large and I would help to set up as many of the music stands as I could. I would then sit at the back through both the choir and orchestra rehearsals. I would watch every one of my brother's (the conductor) movements.

Have you ever wanted to be a post person? When Chris was rehearsing, I would sit at the back doing a vital part in readiness for the forthcoming concerts. I would sit on the floor with a chair in front of me. To my right were boxes and boxes of A4 numbered programme pages in order from front to back. My job was to fold and use what seemed to be a gigantic stapler to secure them together. I even tried to fold the programmes in time to the music. I must have been about seven at the time and I pretended as I did the job methodically that I was a post-lady as I folded each and every one shooting them through the back of a chair as I was the postie. The price of the programme was sixpence (6d in pre-decimal coinage). My wage was a bag of Opal fruit sweets.

Later on, I remember joining the choir and standing in the front line. Linda and Patricia Garnham, Madeleine Rhodes were there, all with their pocket-size skirts and long white boots to their knees. Jack Hawes would play his cello in the orchestra, whilst orchestra leaders included Dave Lewis and Jane Foottit with Alan Stevens playing the trumpet. Peter Willsher was playing the timps.

As I did my little help for Trianon, how proud I am of my big brother for the years of work he has undertaken.

—§—

**JILL CATTO (NÉE FOLEY):** *Memories of the '60s*

*(One of the first members of Trianon, and Orchestra Secretary at a time that the group was expanding.)*

My memories of Trianon are all prior to October 1962, after which I left Ipswich to train in London.

The orchestra was much smaller in those days and I played the recorder alongside Peter Willsher and later a young girl called Catherine. Other people I remember from those days are Maddy Rhodes (née Haste), Marion Botwright, Robin and Rosemary James, John Drake, Colin Moss, Pete Jennings, Brian Cloke, Julian Mallett, Keith Ellis, Carol Long, not forgetting our esteemed leader Dave Lewis.  Many folk were from Northgate but not all.

I'm not sure where all the rehearsals were held but I certainly remember at least one in the home of a member of the orchestra. The importance of rehearsals was so impressed on us that the day my parents moved from Ipswich to Martlesham, I set off for a rehearsal (conducted by John Drake, Chris being at University) from Norwich Road and afterwards left to go to my new home.

One of our early concerts was held in the old Gymnasium at Northgate Girls' School, where my childhood friend Jean Sadler (now Goodson) was our vocal soloist. At least one or more concerts were held in the Music Room of Northgate Boys' School, where I particularly remember we played Haydn's *Toy Symphony* – complete with various sound effects!

Finally, my most vivid memory was when Chris went off to Leeds University in October 1961. During my final year in the orchestra, I received many phone calls from Leeds with lists of jobs that Chris wanted done by myself, together with lists of jobs to pass on to other people!  Calls were lengthy and sometimes interrupted by Mr. Doolan at Kesgrave Manual Telephone Exchange, telling us to clear the line because my father had an important call coming through!

—§—

## ROSEMARY HUMPHRIES (NÉE JAMES): *Trianon across the years*

*(A former member and Secretary of the Trianon Orchestra)*

Ok, it's around 1964. At 16, I was Secretary for the Trianon Orchestra, well before 'choir' days. My main task was to find rehearsal venues – an interesting baptism into the adult world.

The venue I recall most is St Helen's School, Ipswich. My memory is of a typical Edwardian school with an amazing southerly view from the Hall. We were spread out a bit, as we had to fit lengthways in the long narrow hall.

I still 'see' everyone there - Dave Lewis the leader, Mr and Mrs Barrell, Graham Ranson, my brother Robin, Janet Oldham with her oboe, to name just a few.

I recall with a smile when Richard Jones and I (1st and 2nd Flute) had 64 bars' rest. We counted carefully. However ... the piece ended and we hadn't come in! I remember Richard's slight tilt of the head and raised eyebrow to me. Sadly, we lost Richard not long after this which I remember with great sadness.

One of our concert venues was the hall above the Co-op in Carr Street. The piece we played had a dramatic cymbal crash almost at the end. Peter, our able percussionist, gathered his cymbals, all to the 'ready'... Go the cue from Chris! However, he got his jacket caught in the cymbals and the sound was a dull thud. Chris, you were at a distinct advantage as you had your back to the audience. The rest of us had to stifle giggles and tears, which I remember being painful and so funny! We had to plough on and not disintegrate into a Portsmouth Symphonia sound-alike!

Music-making has such power to give enjoyment, achievement, memories and - always - a lot of fun. The camaraderie and the shared special as well as funny moments are precious, and how they have endured over time is proof of this.

—§—

## CHRISTINE RANSON (NÉE BOOTHER): *Trianon memories*

*(A former member of the Trianon Orchestra and Choir)*

I passed my Grade 5 violin exam in the Summer of 1963, and was now eligible to join the Orchestra. I enjoyed settling in, making new friends and performing in the next concerts.

The Christmas Concert on January 11th 1964 was the most memorable. Graham Ranson, who had led the cello section from the early days, asked me if I would like to go to see the film *West Side Story* with him the following week. Naturally I said 'Yes'. I was very flattered as he had a prominent part in this concert, performing a Vivaldi Cello Concerto with the orchestra and in the String Quartet with Dave Lewis, Chris Green and Philip Young. As well as playing in the second violins I was also a founder member of the newly-formed Trianon Choir which gave its first performance that same evening.

As I was still at school studying for "A" levels my parents restricted my dates with Graham to weekends only, but were happy for me to take part in musical activities on other days. Graham saw an opportunity here and also joined the choir so that we could meet more often. He first sang in the basses in the Summer Concert on July 22nd 1964.

When Chris became more ambitious for the Choir with the introduction of joint works for Choir and Orchestra; those of us who were in both had to choose which one to continue. Graham and I chose the orchestra and our extra opportunities to meet at Choir rehearsals stopped. Our relationship thrived though, and we have recently celebrated our Golden Wedding.

—§—

## MADDY RHODES: *The 1960s*

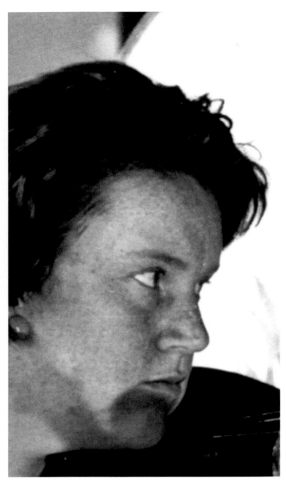

I remember Jimmy James who was Head Teacher of Priory Heath Junior School, which is doubtless why the children from that primary school featured so often in our concerts. Jimmy was accompanist to Ipswich Choral Society, although I didn't know that until I joined them after I'd started teaching back in Ipswich. His two children joined Trianon and he was one of the parental/ avuncular adults who helped the enthusiastic young musicians to establish themselves and learn the ropes of running an organisation.

I remember performing in the Ipswich Art Gallery and the Ipswich Co-op Hall, and it was a concert in the latter to which we first invited the Mayor of Ipswich. I remember thinking we'd really arrived!

Peter Willsher (the first Treasurer of Trianon) remembers his parents taking the ticket money home on the bus after concerts and counting it all on the dining room table. No Paypal, BACS or cashless society in those days! Social events in the 60s included BBQs on Nacton Shore.

Thelma Gilmour also became a key member of the Trianon Choir during the 1960s.

—§—

# CHAPTER THREE

# THE SEVENTIES

*During which the United Kingdom is faced with a number of crises that, in turn, affect the working and domestic lives of its population. Trianon makes its first visit to mainland Europe and its first appearances at the Ipswich Civic College and Royal Hospital School. The Group organises the first of a series of regional music competitions and ends the decade with its 21st Anniversary Concert.*

The Swinging Sixties had passed some of us by and it was a working life that presented itself. By the end of the 1960s, Trianon had a growing orchestra and choir. This made some of the Ipswich venues too small for the purpose of presenting major concerts. It was time for change and that meant finding larger spaces. The Assembly Hall of the Ipswich Civic College (which had opened a few years earlier) and the Assembly Hall of the Royal Hospital School provided solutions, and programmes were designed accordingly.

Conducting of the first programme at the Ipswich Civic College was shared by three people – one of whom, student and Trianon violist Philip Young, conducted his own set of songs from *The Tempest*. The programme was a mix of carols, music for brass, Prokofiev's *Peter and The Wolf* and the curious but fascinating *Choral Fantasia* by Beethoven. Looking back and reviewing that programme, it is difficult not to feel bemused by the eclectic mix and lack of structure in its composition. The same can be said of programmes that followed in that year. The other conductor was Russell Hawes, a music student and bass member from the Trianon choir.

Adrian Brown – then a student at Northgate Grammar School and leader of the orchestra by this time - made his first appearance as conductor sharing the podium with me in the April concert. This was another strange mix of works from the baroque to contemporary, including a newly-written *Choral Suite* by the local composer and member of Trianon's cello section, Jack Hawes.

Trianon has always had members who have composed music and in the sixty years of its existence, the choir and orchestra have variously given premieres of new original works or arrangements by them. Jack had great

"Cartoon by Ipswich-based, Daily Express cartoonist Giles, set in the Buttermarket record shop 'Murdock's'. The statue of Giles's most famous character, Grandma, stands outside the Corn Exchange." Credit: Giles / Daily Express/ Express syndication.

"I fear a lot of mummies and daddies are going to get LP Beatle records for Christmas."

*Daily Express, December 12, 1963*

**OPPOSITE TOP LEFT** *"Sir Malcolm Arnold, former President of Trianon whose **English Dances** performed at the Ipswich Gaumont had a great impact on Chris and are still performed by Trianon."*

"Second tour to Germany in 1972. Harry Asef, our German guide, standing in the centre-left of the photo."

"Adrian Brown, violinist, leader, conductor and composer."

"Jack Hawes (left), cellist, pianist and composer, and Graham Ranson (right)."

"Philip Young, violinist and one of Trianon's early conductors."

kwise: 1: Jack Larter. 2: Chris Hollis. 3: Tim Grant. 4: Roger Steward. 5: John Hannah. 6: Peter Willsher. 7: David Dames. 8: Nigel Jay. 9: Thelma Gilmour. 10: David Beaton. 11: / Asef. 12: Geoffrey Webb. 13: Barbara Heath. 14: Pat Garnham. 15: Malcolm Burren. 16: Linda Cheshire (née Garnham) 17: Celia Godson. 18: Gillian Berry (née Dawes). 19: Alan ?ns. 20: John Barratt (Trianon's current Choir Secretary). 21: Jack Hawes. 22: Charles Paterson. 23: Peter Bumstead. 24: Tim Sewell. 25: Marcus Bennett. 26: Tony Coles. 27: Lewis ?. 28: Chris Green. 29: Janet Dann. 30: Christine Day (née Burren). 31: Sue Harrison (née Hewlett). 32: Susan Debenham.33: Christine Ranson (née Boother). 34: Myrna Hannah. adeleine Rhodes (née Haste).36: Jane Foottit. 37: Jill Horsbrugh. 38: Penny Armstrong. 39: Elizabeth Dickson. 40: Marilyn Mitcham (née Sagar)."

talent both as a pianist as well as cellist, and his style of writing found favour amongst Trianon's musicians. He had worked in Ipswich for much of his life, but composing had played a great part in his life. The *Three English Lyrics* for *a capella* choir had already been premiered in 1968 and was to be one of a number of works he composed during his long period of membership.

Through its early years, members of Trianon had presented concerts in local churches, often supporting fund-raising efforts. Skimming the locations of early venues, reference can be found to local Ipswich churches of: St Thomas, Landseer Road, St Nicholas, Chantry Methodist Church, St Mary-le-Tower, St John's and Museum Street Methodist. Further afield, members visited Battisford, Dedham Parish Church and Wesley Methodist Church (Cambridge). In 1970 Trianon contributed to the 700th anniversary of St Matthew's Church, Ipswich with a programme of Renaissance choral music - repertoire which we rarely now perform, even in Community concerts. How tastes have changed.

Amongst the other Trianon musical "voices" to be heard for the first time in this decade was a work by Adrian Brown - violinist, conductor and now composer whose work *Thaw* was premiered at the Royal Hospital School in September 1970. One composer whose music makes a rare appearance in a 1971 programme is Benjamin Britten. Of course, there had been works like *A Ceremony of Carols* included in our programmes, but I find the relative neglect somewhat surprising. Thinking back, it may be that the close geographical proximity of Britten - he was still alive - meant that many members of Trianon had variously taken part as children in premieres of works such as *St Nicolas* and *Noye's Fludde*, and apart from orchestral works like *Simple Symphony*, *Soirees Musicales* and *Matinees Musicales*, the compositions were not always appropriate to the resources of Trianon at the time.

Gradually programme content was changing to include larger scale works. So, for example in 1970 the choir and orchestra combined for a performance of Beethoven's *Mass in C*. The orchestra was large enough to programme symphonies from the Classical period such as Haydn's *Oxford Symphony*, two symphonies by Schubert and Borodin's Symphony No 3. Ralph Vaughan Williams and Malcolm Arnold were two more modern composers that were to feature regularly in programmes - largely because they had written many works with non-professional performers in mind. The former's *Serenade to Music* makes a programme appearance in a 1969 concert and has, since then, become something of a "signature" work for the Group, featuring in both Golden and Diamond Jubilee programmes. Careful readers will recall the connection with Vaughan Williams's *Serenade* that stems back to my years as a student in Leeds.

As far as Malcolm Arnold was concerned, I first encountered his music as a youngster when I was taken by my godmother to an Ipswich Civic Concert at the Ipswich Gaumont Theatre (now the Ipswich Regent). Sir Adrian Boult conducted the London Philharmonic Orchestra in Arnold's *English Dances*. This would have been mid-1950s. Arnold had been Principal Trumpeter in the LPO until a few years previously and had relinquished the post in favour of composing. The tunefulness and vibrancy of these eight dances made them immediately appealing and I would seek out other music by the same composer whenever it became available. I recall purchasing an "EP" (that is an "Extended Play" vinyl record playing at 45rpm) from a record shop in the Buttermarket, Ipswich having "auditioned" the piece by listening to it in the shop. After all, these were the days when you could spend an entire afternoon asking the assistant to play you a particular recording before purchasing it. That recording was of Arnold's score for a new film called *The Sound Barrier* which, I believe, was filmed in part at Felixstowe.

It was not long before other film scores came my way including *Hobson's Choice* (1953), *The Belles of St Trinian's* (1954) and, of course, the big one - *Bridge over the River Kwai* (1957). I was entirely hooked by the way Arnold produced memorable tunes and the colourful orchestration. Little did I know at the time, that our paths would cross in the 1970s when I became Chairman of the National Association of Youth Orchestras of which he was President, and then again many years after that when he accepted the position as President of Trianon. Trianon's encounters with the composer's music start in 1967 with the *Three Sea Shanties for wind quintet*, followed in 1971 with the *Trevelyan Suite for wind quintet* (a work written for one of his daughters and the college at the University of Durham) and *John Clare Cantata* (reflecting Arnold's Northampton roots), then in 1973 with his Symphony No 2. It was music that suited an extrovert body of players as befitted the public persona of its composer. Little did I know then of the anguish behind that mask.

A review of *The Belles of St Trinian's* just about sums up the approach to his music at that time:

> Most people's memory of the St Trinian's films dates from their
> own youth, when the wonderful indiscipline of the tearaways and the
> debauched indifference of the staff had them longing for their own
> school to be run along similar lines... (Radio Times Guide to Films, 2017)

It is now 1970 and Trianon is about to make its first visit to mainland Europe. To say we planned everything would be wrong. The trip was underwritten, in part, by the West German Government which was spending considerable sums of money in promoting trips to the country, which included visits to sights of political (aka politically sensitive) importance. The steering team centred around three of the Trianon organisation, Janet Dann (alto and administrator), Maddy Rhodes (soprano) and Ivan Gilson (violin). It attracted a large response from both orchestra and choir members. Little did we know of the perils ahead of us as we made our way to Harwich and embarked - complete with coaches - on our way to the Hook of Holland and to Detmold in Westphalia. Ahead of us were four concerts that had been organised by the German "Land" (i.e. County of Lippe). Our hosts would include Herr Harry Asef (who had made his presence very much felt some time earlier in Suffolk) and Fraulein Hildegard Pörtner.

The visit started with an evening reception in one of the old town buildings when drinks - including a very fizzy Cola-equivalent drink called Sinalco - flowed freely. It was not the Sinalco, rather the alcoholic drinks imbibed by the brass players that started the problem. Before the evening had ended, they were merry, and the merriment increased when fresh air hit them as they exited the building. By now, other members of the party were wondering whether they had made a serious mistake in ever deciding to come, especially when one trumpet player had to be retrieved from a box hedge outside the host venue. Not a good start.

Things did improve as we encountered for the first time some of the concert venues organised for our performances. All of them were in spa towns which meant that the audiences were largely ageing Germans taking the local waters. Now, if you have never experienced those waters, dear reader, can I advise you strongly to desist. The procedure is that you sip mouthfuls of salty brine with a low strength and proceed through various points to a gut-wrenching 100 percent proof that can cause the expellation of air from pretty well every orifice that you have and some that you never knew existed – and we had to play in this atmosphere!

The first hall was a magnificent edifice of modern design. We gingerly made our entrance on to the stage, settled down for a rehearsal and, as the first bars echoed round the hall, the side doors opened and we were faced by many men wearing very formal uniforms. Gradually the players and singers came to a halt. Who were these men? It turned out that they were concert hall attendants, but the formality and overpowering uniforms were somewhat daunting.

Bigger surprises were to come. The programme started with the National Anthems of both West Germany and the United Kingdom. That was fine. Everything was ready to go, but I felt an urgent need after the waters - or was it the Sinalco - to go to the toilet. Five minutes before the start, and the door of the loo got stuck. Cries of help produced little result until someone must have heard the cries, and came to my aid. It took five people to extract me from the loo, and never have the National Anthems been performed on such a cushion of air than on this occasion.

Surprise and pleasure got heaped up on the visit, not least by the accommodation provided for us. The hostel might have been of brutalist construction with its concrete exterior, but staying in the countryside with almost four-star facilities was not what we expected. Neither were we prepared for the warm reception from the residents who turned out to be an Order of nuns. This was, in effect, a nunnery. But wait - another problem: the nuns were not dressed monastically. This was an institution where T-shirts and jeans were the order of the working day and so separating - yes - the brass from the German hosts was the next challenge, and with notices being given out each morning by Janet Dann, the instructions "to behave" became more insistent as the days wore on. I think it was also on this trip that one of the party - the budding Trianon version of Sir Colin Davis, Adrian Brown, nearly got himself drowned in the local swimming pool. Thankfully for Trianon and the world of music, he survived.

The afternoon concerts switched venues for four days and included a memorable performance on a bandstand in one of the Kurparks - the outdoor spaces where residents and visitors could sit or take curative walks along the paths between brine hedges and imbibe the smell. This particular performance was on the stage of a concert bowl in the middle of one of these parks, during which the heavens opened and, accompanied by thunder and lightning, Trianon musicians had to make a very fast exit. But what an experience!

It was a very tired but fascinated group of musicians who finally saw the lights of Felixstowe and Harwich appear in the early dawn as we returned to the United Kingdom, vowing that we would go again - and we did, but that is another story for later in this book.

I had changed jobs during the early 1970s, forsaking the College of Education and its oppressive regime for one of the new Polytechnics in North London. This meant a commute every day by car although, looking back, the teaching schedule was not as demanding as it would become later on. The Polytechnic was a large institution where students were free to express themselves, as they had already shown by sabotaging a visit by the then Secretary of State for Education, one Margaret Thatcher MP, and occupying the Director's Office. The years spent at this institution (now part of a well-known University) were stimulating, but it was the combination of us now having a young son (born in 1971) and the challenge of the commute that meant I was to change jobs a second time in the decade.

If this was in any doubt, then the oil crisis of the mid-1970s was to make that change inevitable. Petrol coupons were issued, and I was uncertain as to whether I could get enough fuel to get to work, let alone come to Trianon rehearsals, and would other members of Trianon be able to travel? Things were getting bad as they had done with the "Three-day Week", when electricity supplies were rationed. Not only did this mean that one had to have a plentiful supply of candles to use in case the lights did not work, but also in planning concerts we were never sure as to whether they would have to be cancelled at the last minute because of such power cuts. In the event, we never did have to cancel, but there was little "swinging seventies" about the time.

Trianon needed to raise some funds- largely to invest in equipment such as music stands and timpani. In our very early days, Trianon had organised jumble sales which produced a small but not insignificant source of income. Now we had a larger target and so during the 1970s there was a series of musical evenings (almost soirées) held at the homes of different members when solos, duos and other ensembles would perform. These were in addition to the major concerts which continued to change in repertoire. In April 1974 we were programming Mendelssohn's Violin Concerto, Bernstein's *Chichester Psalms* and Walton's *Crown Imperial*.

One of the mainstays of the Trianon Choir by now was the contralto, Thelma Gilmour. Thelma taught singing from her home in Dedham and had come to join us. She would often take solo parts but also would take a significant role in training the choir as had others from time to time, namely Russell Hawes and Marilyn Sagar (another member of the Trianon Choir).  By 1976, Thelma's role needed formalising and so Chairman, Frank Dames, wrote to Thelma regularising the position and appointing her (nomenclature in those days was quite sexist) as "Chorus Master".

We returned to Germany in 1972 and despite the fuel crises, again in the mid- 1970s. It was a period of considerable challenge. There were fuel crises and, if I remember, I had to ensure I had enough petrol to get me to work in North London and back again especially since another son had entered the family – heralding his arrival by almost emerging at a pedestrian crossing in the middle of the Essex village of Coggeshall as we tried to get to the local maternity unit in Braintree.

By 1975 I had changed jobs which coincided with the third visit to Germany. We thought we had learnt some lessons from our first visits to Detmold, but this was without the present challenge as to whether the coach firm would have fuel to get us there. Also we had been alerted, as were all British groups visiting mainland Europe, particularly Germany where the UK had army bases, that IRA terrorist groups were active. That meant that we had to be vigilant for security reasons.  With the optimism of relative youth, we embarked - this time from Felixstowe – and set sail for the Hook of Holland and on to West Germany. There were many of the same venues and the same musicians but this time the brass decided to get themselves locked out of the hostel one night and – out of sheer boredom or maliciousness - serenade the Trianon members inside by playing their trumpets in the middle of the woods.

"The refurbished Ipswich Corn Exchange. The Grand Hall (pictured) and Robert Cross Hall created within the volume of the original exchange." Credit: John Field.

"Rehearsal prior to Trianon's inaugural concert at the Ipswich Corn Exchange, 1975."

Enough of that. We came back to Ipswich to a more important event. In September 1975 we gave one of the first concerts in the newly refurbished Ipswich Corn Exchange. Two works were on the programme - Prokofiev's final Symphony (No 7) and Brahms' *A German Requiem*. A new period was ushered in, for we had the nearest thing to a proper concert venue. It held an audience of nearly 800, had a proper stage, a balcony, a wonderful entrance with bar facilities and gathering space (now an area sadly a shadow of its former self having been leased out to a major grocery chain). Of course, there were snags. For example, the managers of the venue discovered to their consternation that before the opening concert, which featured a choir and a major London orchestra, the stage could not accommodate all those resources. I will not tell you what had to be done to make things right, but a Health and Safety enquiry at the time might have led to several prosecutions. Anyway, Trianon was there at the beginning taking part in the opening festivities, without a trace of the smells that had once filled the Corn Exchange.

Competitions continued to be organised for woodwind, and piano. The programming got more adventurous with works like Rachmaninov's *Piano Concerto No 2,* Beethoven's *Missa Solemnis* (conducted by Barry Salmon) and a Viennese evening held at the Ipswich School complete with an invitation to the audience to come along and dance.

*"One of the Trianon tour organisers, Ivan Gilson (right), pictured with Chris Green at the Ipswich Wet Dock".*

If Germany had had enough of us, we certainly had not had enough of Germany and a further trip was organised in 1977. In that year most of the concerts were conducted by Barry Salmon (then Head of Music at one of the local independent schools), or by London-based professional conductor John Lubbock. The opening concert of 1978 heralded the first major themed concert, Merry-go-Round, ending with the first external commission from celebrated conductor and composer of light music (then residing in Stowmarket) Paul Fenoulhet: *The Beatles Medley*. The work had already been played in Germany with great success and that was repeated before a packed-out Ipswich audience. We really did not have to work hard to get those audiences.

So, the 1970s came to a close, but not before we introduced the music of another composer who was and continues to play a significant role in Trianon's life - John Rutter. His *Gloria* for choir and brass was programmed for the January 1979 concert in the Ipswich Corn Exchange. By this time I had got to know John through my appointment as Arts Producer for the newly formed Radio Orwell, one of the first commercial radio stations in the country. That appointment gave me the opportunity to meet and interview so many other musicians including Rostropovich, Penderecki, Benny Goodman, the original Swingle Singers, members of the Academy of St Martin in the Fields, Sir Charles Groves and Sir Alexander Gibson – the latter pair, surely two of the nicest conductors I have had the privilege to meet.

—§—

# TRIPS DOWN MEMORY LANE WITH FRIENDS

**ADRIAN BROWN:** *A tribute to Trianon*

*(Former member, violin leader and composer, professional conductor and a Vice President and Guest Conductor of Trianon)*

My first memory is going to a concert in the old Co-op Hall in the early sixties supporting friends at Northgate. I longed to join the orchestra. Not long ago I found the programme where I had given the pieces marks out of ten!

On joining it became a way of life; not only leading eventually, but having that needed 'chance'. That chance to conduct and perform my own inadequate compositions. It says much for Chris Green's way of working that many enjoyed the opportunities the late sixties had to offer, for me, enhancing my time at the Royal Academy.

Many in the musical fraternity of Suffolk were snooty about Trianon. "Standards, my dear!" It accepted all comers in the ranks. As if every other snobbish group was so wonderful! I learnt much then about how to respect and handle amateur musicians and Youth. Perhaps what not to do; but I was given that 'chance' to develop; that music in Trianon has always been for all. I reflect, too on the variety of repertoire not least the biggest flag waved for British Music. How has this come about? How has it survived? Because of Chris's hypnotic belief in what to do.

Over the years it has been a pleasure to come back and conduct and share my experience. I have been met with much warmth by Trianon as the shade changes from Green to Brown!! I am proud of the music in my home town and it is a shame that my willingness perhaps to celebrate my gratitude to Ipswich music can't be used more. Trianon 'is' Chris, yes, but it is also about those who have stood by him for many years. Long may it continue to make composers and students like me, all those years ago, happy.

—§—

**PETER WILLSHER:** *Trianon Remembered*

*(Former timpanist, pianist and Officer of Trianon, and occasional accompanist now)*

As children of the sixties we inhabited a world full of optimism and opportunities. Looking back now, I have pride that our achievements then laid the foundations for where Trianon is now. We were teenagers together running a group that organised three concerts a year with a few additional chamber concerts. A handful of supportive adults facilitated these activities: Joyce and Bernard Barrell, Bertha Carter, "Jimmy" James, John Parry, not to mention Chris's family. Other than a modest local authority grant, Trianon was self-funding and outgoings never exceeded income from ticket sales.

This pioneering group of intrepid teenagers, some now entering their early twenties, organised a tour to the twinned town of Detmold, years before foreign trips became the norm for youth orchestras. Lengthy negotiations by letter and telephone were the means of making arrangements, not instant internet communication taken for granted today.

Back home, a competition, open to any young pianist living or studying in the region, predated the now well-established BBC Young Musician. Part of the prize, and one of the reasons the idea of a competition evolved, was the opportunity to perform a concerto with the Trianon Orchestra.

Trianon gave us: very happy times; so many musical opportunities; lifelong friends.

--§--

**JENNY TOLE:** *Snapshots*

*(A member of the viola section of the Trianon Orchestra in the early years, a singer who would often take solo roles and a founding member of the Trianon choir. She now lives in Lincolnshire)*

As you grow old, they say,
Memory lengthens, near stays dim.
Good news for me then .....
I'm not there yet.

Almost sixty years ago
Where did we rehearse?
Concerts in the Civic College, the Art
Gallery?
Viola parts going, 'sniff, bow, sniff, bow.'
We shuffled our chairs to the syncopation
And dutifully counted our bars of rest:
One, two, three, four ....thirty, two, three,
four,
In!

Not only the music had its 'delicate'
moments.
Do you remember the delayed second
half?
The conductor – guess who,
Was stuck in the loo!
And where did we wait for a couple,
Working on inter-group co-operation
Between choir and orchestra?
They walked unabashed up the central aisle.

When the choir started
It brought some extra joy, for
It's my better discipline.
But in combined works – consternation!
Should I play or should I sing?
Manoeuvre through the music stands,
Miss the trombone slides,
Wriggle round the timpani
And climb up to the sops.

Trip to Detmold, looked after by the kindly Heinz.
Was it the Exernsteine we climbed?
We must have played and sung,

Spectacular sandstone pillars
But I remember giant, green
With steps up to the view.
Hermannsdenkmal, monument to
We must have played and sung.
Hero warchief, defeater of Romans,
Rising above the Teutobergerwald.
Looking at old photographs.
We were insufficiently impressed by his status
And he became
'Green Hermann, we saw standing all alone',
To the tune of 'Fair Phyllis', by John Farmer.
But impressed enough to remember him!

—§—

## STEFAN ASEF:

*(Stefan's father, Harry Asef, was an invaluable support to Trianon during concert tours to Westphalia in the 1970s. Stefan and his family remain close friends of Chris).*

60 years of Trianon – but I was just about 10 when I first met you. Detmold, my home town in Germany, and Ipswich were talking about becoming twin towns at the time, and quite a few groups were travelling to and fro to build up closer relationships. Among them was the Trianon Music Group, choir and orchestra, and to help them across language barriers my father was asked to accompany them during their visit as an interpreter. My sister and I, being on school holidays, were invited and joined the group on their sightseeing program between concerts and rehearsals – a wonderful time and the beginning of a wonderful friendship.

Although the Detmold/Ipswich twinning did not work out in the end a lot of friendships have lasted. Trianon visited Detmold a few more times over the years – and the Detmold Youth Orchestra also came to Ipswich on several occasions.

Myself, I even lived in Ipswich for six months in 1979/1980 with a great lot of help from Trianon members and other friends we had made, and I still regard Ipswich as a second home and Trianon as a sort of second family even without a musical connection because I never learned an instrument or to sing.

It is the fourth time I have been invited to anniversary celebrations, and I feel deeply honoured that I may attend. All the best to Trianon Music Group, and I would not mind to come again in 10, 20 or even 30 years.

—§—

*"Harry Asef, Stefan's father, pictured in the 1980s"*

**MADDY RHODES:** *The Seventies*

*(Madeleine Haste had become Maddy Rhodes by the third visit to Detmold)*

During the 1970s, I took part in a number of Trianon visits to West Germany, in 1970, 1972, and 1975. I missed the fourth visit in 1977 as I had a 5-month old daughter.

I remember the long hold ups at the Dutch/German border on the first two visits, and all the paperwork handled by our two fatherly coach drivers. We weren't in the EU then. The journeys were a lot easier once the borders were scrapped! And of course I remember the night we left a sleeping member behind when we drove through the night after another party full of sausage and Sinalco – that locally bottled fizzy drink (and Janet Dann was sooooo cross with me for not realising). I think I was more concerned about another member who had imbibed too much German Beer and was also cross with me for some reason.

—§—

# CHAPTER FOUR

# THE EIGHTIES

*During which time Trianon extended its chamber concerts and took an active part in the newly established Ipswich Arts Festival including a series of Saturday morning concerts – celebrated the 21st Anniversary of Trianon's choir and the 25th Anniversary of the orchestra – performed for the first time in the Chapel of the Royal Hospital School and at Snape Maltings – and ended the decade with the formation of a symphonic wind ensemble. During that time there was a search for new rehearsal premises and a brief tenancy of a redundant Ipswich church.*

*"Jeffery Babb in 2016 at his 90th birthday"*

At first glance, it seems like the 1980s were going to be like the 1970s - a continuation of the pattern of three major concerts each year, competitions, and a series of chamber-style programmes delivered in different venues including the homes of families of members. To an extent, that is true, but very few years have passed without some changes to that pattern. In 1980, Trianon welcomed the first appearance of Jeffery Babb as Guest Conductor. Jeffery had been Head of Music at a School in Grimsby, and as Secretary of the National Association of Youth Orchestras he had worked with me. The link extended also to the fact that several current members had moved with their parents from Grimsby, where ICI had production facilities, to Suffolk and had been pupils of Jeffery.

I was always overwhelmed by the energy that Jeffery displayed, and his grasp of orchestral organisation was something to admire. He was to be one of several Guest Conductors during the 1980s, including Professor Peter Aston who became Trianon's second President following the death of Imogen Holst in 1984. Peter, a well-known composer and teacher, held the Chair in

Music at the University of East Anglia and made his conducting debut with Trianon in 1986.

Trianon's commitment to developing the musical talents of young people continued with the competitions that were organised on an occasional basis. Planning and organising these was always a challenge. There were premises to hire that enabled musicians to be heard to the best, juries to be formed from musicians with a national reputation, prize monies to be sought and rules to be finalised. As far as Trianon was concerned, it was hoped that a winner would, from time to time, be found from within Trianon, but since the competition was open to young musicians from across the Eastern region, that meant there were entrants from six counties - Bedfordshire, Cambridgeshire, Essex, Hertfordshire, Norfolk and Suffolk.

Musicians from Trianon always put on a highly creditable display, but no winners emerged from the ranks. Instead we enjoyed successes from a range of regionally-based musicians, many of whom have gone on to develop international careers. The 1981 winner of the Trianon Organ Competition was Anne Page, later to become well known as an organ recitalist and Organist at one of the Cambridge colleges. In the same competition, the runner–up has recently re- emerged as the Chief Executive Officer of Dubai Airport, one of the busiest in the world who, according to the BBC Music Magazine, cited the Trianon Organ Competition as giving him the encouragement to continue studying and playing the organ despite a grueling work schedule.

In 1984, the winner of the string competition was a young Chelmsford violinist, Anthony Marwood, now amongst the top violin soloists in the United Kingdom with numerous BBC Proms appearances and recordings to his credit.

The competitions brought a lot of praise to Trianon, not only for the organisational standards but also for the platform they provided for young talent. However, the writing was on the wall. The competitions needed to attract more prize monies and concert opportunities. As the decade proceeded, other national competitions emerged backed by big prize money. By 1989, when the Trianon String Competition was organised, there were serious issues to be resolved and so this event proved to be the last in the series.

Putting together major concert programmes is always a fascinating, if challenging task. The challenge, to select music that gives a certain uniqueness to Trianon's programming, that are affordable and that can result in the music being sourced. In the 1980s, it was still possible to rely heavily upon the local library system to ensure the borrowing of sets of choral and orchestral music at a very reasonable rate. Failing that, there still existed commercial libraries such as Goodwin and Tabb which would carry

"Howard Dann started in Trianon and is now a professional bassoonist and supplier of hand-crafted bassoon reeds."

"One of many 'Trianon families': Natalie, Howard and Amy Dann pictured in costume for the performance in 1990 of Granpa by Howard Blake. They all subsequently joined the orchestra where their father, Lewis, played the bassoon. Janet, their mother, has been a Chair of Trianon and still sings in the choir."

*"Left: Anne Page, winner of the 1981 Trianon Organ competition and now recitalist, tutor at the Royal Academy of Music and founder and trustee of the Cambridge Academy of Organ Studies. Right: Anthony Marwood, winner of the 1984 Trianon String competition and now violin soloist."*

*"25th anniversary celebration of the Trianon Choir at the Royal Hospital School (September 1988)."*

sets of orchestral music at hire charges that seemed reasonable, although much higher than would be paid to public libraries. The third source was Trianon's own growing library of choral and orchestral sets. This collection represents a considerable investment of money for little return unless, of course, the works are regularly repeated.

During the 1980s, there were names that appeared in the programming for the first time. A name that was, and still is, prominent in Trianon's programmes is that of John Williams. In 1980 Trianon performed music from *Star Wars*, the first episode of which - *A New Hope* - had been shown in cinemas about 3 years previously. Apart from taking my two young sons to see it on its release in the UK, I had already made an acquaintance with John Williams' music when I had to review new LP releases for the local newspaper, the *Ipswich Evening Star*. One of these I had selected as the theme signature tune for a new radio programme which I had taken charge of for Ipswich's first commercial radio station, Radio Orwell. That theme music was for *The Towering Inferno* a film that had starred Steve McQueen. Each week one could hear that pounding theme on Sunday evenings. Little did I know then, that John Williams' music would become a major feature of Trianon's subsequent programmes, with music from the films *Harry Potter, Hook, Jaws, Jurassic Park, Saving Private Ryan, Schindler's List* and *Superman* making their presence felt in the many film programmes that the group has performed.

But if Trianon leaned towards the popular amongst contemporary music, the programming also included works from the major classical repertoire, making full or partial use of the existence of choir and orchestra. In 1983, the group performed Handel's *Messiah* for the first time with distinguished soprano Patricia Rozario amongst the solo line-up. In 1988, it was the turn of Elgar's *The Dream of Gerontius* - probably one of the most moving performances I can recall, making full use of the Royal Hospital School Chapel - and the same composer's *The Musicmakers* at Snape in 1987.

Twice in the 1980s, we find *Carmina Burana* being performed. This was at a time when very few non-professional music groups had the resources to programme it. The first time Trianon performed the work few of the choir really understood what the words were about, since recording companies chose to redact the translation because of the lewdness of some of the poems. However, I am pleased to say that over the years, those members who have remained with the choir or orchestra have gradually learnt the meaning of the texts, and a smile comes to some of their faces more readily when the relevant ones are sung.

One of the criticisms we have had from time to time is that not enough attention has been given to music from the Baroque and Classical periods. This is true, but the justification is based around the scoring. These works were often performed by small ensembles, and the symphonic line-up of Trianon's orchestra would mean excluding a number of players from the performance because their instruments are not required in the scoring. On the positive side, however, works from the baroque periods have, more recently, been programmed in Trianon's community-based concerts when a small string ensemble is available. During the 1980s, there was a notable exception when Bach's *St John Passion* was performed.

One of the challenges that has continually been faced by Trianon is sourcing suitable rehearsal premises. The Ipswich Scout Headquarters had been a valuable location to us during the 1960s and 1970s, but it was sold off. So we had to find other venues. During that period a number of redundant churches in Ipswich had become available, A bold move on Trianon's part was to go into partnership with the Ipswich Historic Churches Trust and Ipswich Borough Council to put St Lawrence Church to good use.

*"The derelict interior of St. Lawrence Church, Ipswich, pictured in the 1980s."*
*Photo credit: John Field*

The challenge was to take the fine historic church with the oldest peal of bells in England and turn it into a rehearsal venue. The state of the building inside was dreadful with a floor far from safe; no heating, no toilets, in fact, a shell of a building which was damp. Cue the ingenuity of Trianon members who, led by Ivan Gilson and Gillian Williams, transformed the church into a viable proposition - or so we thought! A replacement floor was manufactured at Trianon's expense and industrial strength heaters installed for use, but it did not stop members from sweating. not from over exertion, but rather from the damp that seemed to exude from every nook and cranny.

The church started being used for Saturday morning concerts during the summer, organised by Trianon and the newly formed Ipswich Arts Association, but it was the winter months that provided the challenge. St Lawrence and the surrounding area was, for a number of people, rather intimidating at night-time. With rough sleepers choosing the paved graveyard, things began to look bleak again. A murder in that graveyard finally sealed the decision to vacate the church and so another episode in the Trianon story came to an end.

As we came to the end of the 1980s, there was one more development. A newcomer to Suffolk made himself known to me. Major Brian Keeling had been Musical Director of the Blues and Royals Regiment of the Household Guards. He had featured as one of the senior musicians in the British army in many recordings and had also been present when the IRA placed and exploded a bomb on Horse Guards Parade. Several animals and bandsmen were either injured or killed. Brian had now retired from the army and was interested in getting involved with local music. What better way than to ask him to form a symphonic wind band (that is woodwind and brass instruments) under the Trianon banner. This he did and, in 1989, the Symphonic Wind Band gave its first concert in March at the Ipswich Town Hall.

—§—

# TRIPS DOWN MEMORY LANE WITH FRIENDS

**JANET DANN:** *Trianon and Me*

*(A long-time member of Trianon with her husband, Lewis; a former Chairperson of the group and well-known for her literary contributions at Trianon concerts).*

In 1969 on moving to Suffolk we joined Trianon Music Group on its 10th anniversary, Lewis as a bassoonist and I as an alto. The dark magic of Trianon soon had us deeply involved – tours to Germany, musical evenings with the Friends of Trianon, hosting the annual carol singing – and within the next decade Lewis was editing Trianon News (which we turned out by hand on a Roneo duplicator) and I was General Secretary.

When I look back at the tours, the competitions, the special events, new works and the sheer range and volume of the repertoire which I have been able to experience, it's hard to remember how we managed when three children came along to add to the fun! I do remember that our first daughter Natalie slept obligingly, at two weeks old, in a side room as I compèred an Ipswich Arts Festival event in the Town Hall Council Chamber!

In due course they all took their place in Trianon Orchestra, so all 5 of us were regular members in the '90s, and the continuation of music in their lives is the legacy from Chris' original intention in forming the Group all those years ago. My son Howard, following in Lewis' footsteps, is a professional bassoonist and said recently:

'When I was starting out, that experience of playing such a diversity of repertoire and the discipline of getting it right quickly gave me a head start in orchestral playing which has proved invaluable.'

Chris' drive is and has always been phenomenal. We have had our fallings out over the years, but our friendship has stood the test of time; my one regret is that particular circumstances prevented me from spending a longer time as Chair of the Group. But here we are, still trying to recruit tenors, still asking for tea volunteers, wrangling rehearsal venues and taking up challenges so that we can go on making ever more music.

Oh, the tales I could tell...but my lips are sealed, and my word count is up...

—§—

## MARK BONNEY: *Trianon*

*(A member in the early life of the Trianon Orchestra together with his sister, Alison. Mark helped organise early rehearsals and events. He is now Dean of Ely Cathedral).*

We moved as family to Ipswich in 1964 when my father took up the headship of St Margaret's Church of England Primary School, a post he held for 22 years. I was 7 then, and it must have been some 7 or 8 years later that I joined Trianon, and over the next few years sang and played in many exciting concerts. My abiding memory is of the infectious enthusiasm that Chris Green brought to all that we did, and through that gaining exposure to some exciting musical repertoire. It's a very long time ago now! But I do, for some reason, particularly recall Trianon giving me my first experience of *Carmina Burana*, and have loved it ever since. I also have vivid memories of *Flos Campi* with Timothy Grant playing solo viola, and a somewhat hairy experience of playing first flute in Walton's *Henry V Suite*.

My sister Alison played horn regularly in the orchestra (she sadly died in 2002). What I know we both gained from those days was a great love of music-making and that camaraderie that comes from working towards a common goal. My memory is that there was a wide age range of people taking part in Trianon, but there were particularly a lot of us (then) young people, and that Trianon played a formative part in our musical (and social!) lives. And for that I am hugely grateful, and have been delighted that Chris's enthusiasm has carried on for 60 years!

—§—

**NIGEL KING:** *Happy Memories!*

*(Long-time member of the double bass section of the Trianon Orchestra and currently Vice-Chairperson).*

There must be many ways that people have been drawn in to the choir or orchestra of the Trianon Music Group. Family connection must be a favourite. My cousins were members of the group and their father was also involved as Honorary Treasurer.

One day I received a telephone call from my cousin, Susan King, saying the TMG orchestra needed double bass players. I had not been playing that long but the orchestra must have been desperate, and I couldn't have been that bad as 50 years on (approximately - somebody with a collection of all the programmes should be able to find out when I first played) I am still involved.

How can I forget explaining to my parents that my mother's car would be required to take myself and instrument to Ipswich from Chelmsford, where we lived at that time, probably eight times over a four-week period? Each journey would involve removing the passenger seat from her Austin A35 to transport the bass! What was at the end of the journey? Six flights of stairs to the third floor of the Ipswich Scouts H.Q. - a good size room that took all the orchestra and, with a squeeze, the choir as well for joint rehearsals. These rehearsals were accompanied by gymnastic rhythms from the floor above. Happy memories!

—§—

**MADDY RHODES:** *The 80s*

I remember scrubbing the floor in St Lawrence's church (where incidentally I had been a member of the church choir). My mum came to help too. I don't remember the dates but we only used that church for a couple of years, didn't we?

I remember the big heaters there which roasted you if you sat near them. I don't know how we managed refreshments but McDonald's was close. I do remember having to light the boiler in the Scout HQ kitchen, however. It involved getting up close with a match – and everyone entrusted to make the tea was terrified of it!

I also remember how the whole place rattled and shook on nights when we shared it with the gymnasts! And there wasn't a lot of space in the library for the choir – and incidentally where were the books?

Remember the night we were locked out of the Scout HQ? A very obliging PC happened to come past and with the aid of someone's new-fangled Barclaycard managed to get us in. He was either very trusting or we managed a completely believable story. Was it the silver-tongued Chris I wonder? (It wouldn't have been CG passing over his plastic, I'm sure).

—§—

# CHAPTER FIVE

# THE NINETIES

*A time of new challenges in seeking new venues, working with composers and a new President. Before the end of the decade, there was planning for the new millennium - and whether Trianon plans would be scuppered by the Millennium "bug" that would bring life as we know it to a halt. Before that Trianon members would dice with death as they navigated Dutch scenic routes on a coach best suited to school trips.*

If the Victorian age is often dubbed the Roaring Nineties, then there was something of a roar about Trianon's programming in the 1990s.

The final work of 1989 marked the 30th Anniversary concert at the Ipswich Corn Exchange - by now an important venue in the major concert programmes of Trianon. Carl Orff's *Carmina Burana* had to have another outing. After all, some members who had experienced the previous version were a bit older now and were in a better position to appreciate the text set by Orff. Those sensual and risqué verses originating from an Austrian monastery were medieval porn, but now got a lusty rendition from Trianon members.

So into a new decade and another challenge. For the first time, Trianon managed to stage three concerts in 24 hours with the first visit to Chelmsford's Riverside Ice and Leisure Complex on a Friday evening and, as some have often observed, Trianon does not always help itself by minimising that challenge. Actually, there was more than one challenge.

The first: to get an orchestra and choir to Chelmsford from Ipswich on time on a Friday evening with sufficient time to set up and have a brief rehearsal. Achieved. The second: to introduce to the musicians composer Howard Blake who was going to narrate – for the first time - his new work *Grandpa*. There had been some "dry runs" with me beforehand at Howard's London flat for which we were joined by a young singer from Essex (recruited after auditions). Achieved.

The third challenge was to get the sound right in a vast barn of a Leisure

Centre; and would we get an audience? The answer was a partial "Yes" on both counts and it was a reasonably contented bunch of musicians who set off back to Ipswich at the end of this away-day Concert. But the challenges had not finished because we had scheduled an afternoon Junior Pops concert in the Ipswich Corn Exchange on the following day at 2.30pm, followed by the full-blown programme at 7.30pm. Achieved, but with vague mutterings of "Never again", and so that was that.

The link with Howard Blake once again emphasised the importance Trianon has always placed upon working with living composers. In retrospect it has usually been a good one. Contemporary composers can be very generous but some of them write music which is best suited to chamber-size choirs in scoring that places great emphasis on rehearsing with skilled sight readers and those who can take solo parts. With the Trianon schedule that kind of work would pose insurmountable problems and, apart from that, there is the challenge of getting audiences to respond.

In the same case of some orchestral music, the scoring can prove a challenge with composers requiring a range of instruments that can only be assembled when one is operating in a major centre where such resources might be readily available.

We have been very fortunate in having a number of composers within Trianon and many of them have contributed works which we have programmed. There are, of course, some from outside the Group who got away! I was hoping that I might be able to persuade Malcolm Williamson (the Australian composer who was Master of The Queen's Music) to compose for us, but a radio interview with him was sufficient to prove to me that it might not be such a good idea and, as events turned out, how right I was. One only has to read his biography to find the reasons. A well-known critic offered me an introduction to Sir Arthur Bliss (then Master of the Queen's Music), but he passed away before the introduction took place. Sadly, by the time Sir Malcolm Arnold became Trianon's President, he was too ill to contemplate writing anything for the Group, but that has been more than offset by the marvellous legacy he left with his instrumental, orchestral and film music which we have mined on many occasions.

Back then to the Roaring Nineties. Records show that in April 1990 we gave our first concert at Snape Maltings. That must have been a brave move to consider a concert in that venue - expensive as it was – for a concert in April which always means a smaller-sized audience. As it happens, it must have been successful because Snape became a regular venue for subsequent years in 1991, 1993, 1995, and 1996. Entering on to the large staging area for the first time was daunting, especially if one remembered in whose footsteps one was following, but to have good backstage facilities - in sharp contrast to the Ipswich Corn Exchange - was a boon. The principal Dressing Room was magnificent and brought back memories of the time I had prepared to do a radio interview in that space. Having set up the equipment I went to collect the artist whom I was to interview only to return to the dressing room to discover a man asleep on the sofa. He turned out to be distinguished American clarinettist, Bennie Goodman.

But, at the time, we had another thing on our collective mind - the challenge of finding rehearsal space for our Ipswich meetings. St Lawrence Church had been pressed into service and it needed to be put on the map. So, in July 1990, Trianon organised a series of Saturday morning Coffee Concerts which turned out to be very popular even though St Lawrence Church got no warmer and was going to prove a far-from-pleasant location for Trianon.

In the first year of the new decade with the Choir and Orchestra presenting a concert in September 1990 to mark the 50th Anniversary of the Battle of Britain there begins a trend in programming that remains to the present - the emphasis upon thematic concerts. This, like many other examples in this book, reflects the way Trianon's Music Committee works. My role as Artistic Director is to provide sample programmes from which members debate and decide. The first step that the Music Committee has to make is to decide whether or not there is to be a theme to the programme.

Meanwhile, the Trianon Symphonic Wind Band was making a journey to Chelmsford to perform at the Civic Theatre. The thematic format for choir and orchestra continued with *Sounds Fantastic* (January 1991), and we even managed to persuade musicians to perform the programme twice on the same day. *Sounds Familiar* was the title and it provided an open invitation to programme many popular classics. So, the January series seemed to be set for what followed in 1994 with *New Year's Music Magic*... and so on.

I have always been well supported by the knowledge which members of Trianon's Music Committee bring to the table. Alright, some ideas have been rather whacky but when there is a major commemorative year, you can be sure that members will come along with some good ideas. Mozart got the treatment in 1991 when players and singers from Trianon gave the same programme eight times in places such as Bury St Edmunds, Ipswich and Felixstowe. *Purcell 300* followed in 1995 with six outings and, in 1997, Schubert, Mendelssohn and Brahms got the same treatment with *Three Romantics*.

At the beginning of this journey I recalled how the Ipswich Corn Exchange would often resonate to the sounds of the Ipswich Choral and Orchestral Societies giving their seasonal concerts accompanied by the smell of flowers and rotting vegetables. The "old" Corn Exchange had been used as a flower and vegetable market on certain days of the week, and the smells lingered on. I am not sure whether I ever heard the Ipswich Choral Society

*"Pat Garnham (soprano), one of the soloists at both the 40th and forthcoming 60th anniversary concerts."*

*"Chris and Lenie van der Wal, president of Trianon's Dutch partner choir, l'Espérance."*

*"Left: Around the table of the Christchurch Street dining room where many hours have been spent by Trianon's Management and Music committees. Right: Frank Dames presenting Maddy Rhodes with a Giles cartoon of 'Grandma' at Trianon's 40th anniversary."*

perform Vaughan Williams' *A Sea Symphony* in that building, but in 1991 Trianon decided to programme the work even though the performance space with a full audience (those were the days) was not generous. Six years later we returned to the same work in the more spacious Chapel at the Royal Hospital School, but again there was the challenge of being able to hear the same work three times in reverberant succession with the infamous (and splendid) acoustic, meaning that every silent beat had to be judged to perfection. When better to do that than in a performance of Saint-Saens' *Organ Symphony* which got an outing in September 1994 with Peter Crompton, then Director of Music, playing the wonderful organ? The only thing lacking was a defibrillator because some of the audience were visibly and physically moved by the point when the organ joins with the orchestra in the "big" tune. Peter had mischievously ratcheted up the sound to make the most of the acoustics and did it vibrate!

And, on the subject of vibrations, Trianon took a bold decision to programme William Walton's *Belshazzar's Feast*. Some thought this was a step too far with the challenges of double choirs, semi-chorus and two additional bands, but with the warm acoustic provided by Snape Maltings, we carried it off successfully in 1993. Another Biblical epic followed in 1996 with Mendelssohn's *Elijah*. I recall our new President, Professor Peter Aston, coming backstage after the performance of *Belshazzar's Feast* and saying that he had never thought that a collection of non-professional players would bring off the score so well! Praise indeed for the Trianon musicians - players and singers alike.

So, as we approached the end of Trianon's fourth decade what else was there new for us? Movie Music- ah yes. Now in the 1990s music from the movies was restricted to big hits like *Gone With The Wind* and *Star Wars*, but we managed to broaden the choice with excerpts from films such as *The Tales of Beatrix Potter* (performed with members of the Chelmsford Ballet Company dancing) and *Murder on the Orient Express*.

In January 1998 we programmed the first *Trianon at the Movies* programme, and since then have continued to explore this rich vein of repertoire. It might seem an easy task, but actually sourcing music that can be hired at a reasonable price has become ever more of a challenge. Publishing Companies now realise they have a valuable commodity with works like *Gladiator, Harry Potter* and so on. Gone are the days when I visited EMI offices in Charing Cross Road to meet someone who indicated a cardboard box in the corner and invited me to take what scores I wanted from it. With no carrying case, I managed to plunder copies of scores from *Tales of Beatrix Potter, Four Weddings and a Funeral, Murder on the Orient Express* and much more. Alright, they may not have been the original composer scores, but were photocopies. However, they have remained a cherished addition to my library of scores and a reminder that by now most Hollywood studios were sending such scores and orchestral parts to landfill sites in an act of artistic vandalism.

So, to another Anniversary. In September 1999 we would celebrate Trianon's Fortieth but not before we had introduced *The Trianon Ipswich Prom* in the September of the previous year with the usual flag waving and renditions of *Jerusalem* and *Land of Hope and Glory.* If I recall, the 40th Anniversary was a pleasant but restrained affair with Elgar's *The Musicmakers* coupled with Vaughan Williams's *Serenade to Music.* What is so good to remember is that three of the four soloists - Pat Garnham, Maggie McDonald and Tim Gillott – would be around to sing with Trianon in their 60th Anniversary in 2019.

In the last year of the decade, members of Trianon once again embarked from Harwich for the Hook of Holland, and our first visit to the Netherlands as guests of our new partner choir, l'Espérance. l'Espérance has a proud history going back to 1892, led by its energetic Secretary, Lenie van der Wal, and conductor Wim Madderom. The visit proved a pleasant and entertaining one.

The planning of the trip had, we thought, been quite thorough but - as on the most well-planned of occasions - we had not looked round some corners to see what was going to challenge us. The first thing was a coach driver who was obviously unfamiliar with his coach, having let down the hydraulic suspension of his vehicle for the voyage over to the Hook. He did not allow time to pump it up again and the coach got grounded on the ramp leading off the ferry, much to the frustration and increasing annoyance of the ferry's staff who had started letting vehicles on for the return voyage.

That was only the beginning of a succession of problems, for the driver, having finally managed to jack the coach up and motored on to the quayside, obviously did not appreciate the height restrictions found on some Continental motorways. I should explain that the vehicle we had hired was a double decker, and that was going to prove a fascinating experience later on.

We had chosen what seemed a logistically good, reasonably priced location for our stay on the Rotterdam ring road. The restaurant may have been a bit small for the party and the traffic noise slightly intrusive, but it did mean we were well located for our various journeys. However, after the first night, many of the members started complaining about the noise of footsteps during the night. The bedrooms led to an outside passageway- very convenient, but it echoed. Gradually, the explanation emerged: the hotel was a favourite stop for long-distance lorry drivers and obviously was well frequented by the passing sex workers of Rotterdam. It was their footsteps that were heard during the night.

Back to our trusted vehicle. One of the first concerts was scheduled for a church in central Rotterdam. Our driver, helped by our usually on-the-ball coach courier, Ivan Gilson, set out for the afternoon rehearsal, but could not find the way into the road where the church was located. We could see the building, and probably the most sensible thing to have done was to stop, disembark and walk the final distance, but we had a lot of instruments. Eventually we reached our destination, well behind schedule which meant that the evening meal at a local hotel was late. The restaurant was under-staffed and Trianon members ended up by serving in order to try to regain some time.

It was becoming like one of those nightmare dreams, where one cannot extricate oneself from a series of impending disasters. There was more to come. The meal finished, we had to race back to the church - on foot mercifully- by which time we were already late for the scheduled time start. The concert proceeded without incident - or at least, if there was one, none of us noticed, and we finally made it back to the night-time encounters of Rotterdam's suburbs.

Our meeting with the members of l'Espérance was, as was soon evident, going to be a friendly and biblical one. Each concert started with the singing of a psalm as is customary in Dutch Reformed churches, and the combined choirs mingled with few problems under the joint direction of myself and Wim Madderom, their conductor. His conducting style - expansive and very physical - provided a great change from mine and our singers responded with enthusiasm. The players who accompanied us continued in their usual somewhat cautious approach, but it was great to have them with us.

So, to the final encounter with that vehicle. We had gone to visit the UNESCO World Heritage site at Dordrecht - the windmills that one often sees on television. Our guide had asked us whether we wanted to take the scenic or direct route back to Rotterdam. The former was chosen. What had not been established is the nature of that route and the vehicle which was going to take us. Suffices to say that every time we approached a bridge on the motorway our driver would slow down in anticipation of the coach's roof being sliced off! This time he was to face something altogether more of a challenge.

The route back to home base was along a single-track road flanked by dykes on either side. Sitting on the upper deck of the coach required a head for heights. The journey was slow, but it was going to get slower for we were to meet a tractor coming in the opposite direction. What to do: it seemed that farm vehicles had right of way and so the coach had to back up along this track. Exit four Trianon volunteers who shouted instructions to the driver as he backed down to a suitable turning point. I am not sure whether photos were taken - if they were, they would be a suitable record of a journey into hell.

Frightened? You bet. But it did not stop the trips to the Netherlands and there was yet more fun to come.

The decade had ended for me when, in late 1994, a letter plopped through my letter box. Opening it, I discovered it was from the Lord Chancellor's Office saying that I had been nominated for the Order of the British Empire. The citation read that the award was for services to mental health, and to the arts in East Anglia. Would I accept? I was bound to secrecy, but of course I consulted my family and my father with whom I had been reunited. The announcement was made on 31 December through the official London journal, and it was followed by radio and newspaper enquiries prior to the press release on New Year's Day.  What followed seemed surreal - the investiture in 1995 with a family trip to Buckingham Palace and being received into the presence of Her Majesty The Queen accompanied by music from the Gallery of The Ballroom, and then photos outside in the courtyard and a meal at The Savoy.

*"Chris receiving his OBE from the Queen".*

# TRIPS DOWN MEMORY LANE WITH FRIENDS

**MARGARET McDONALD:** *Memories of Trianon.*

*(Former member of the Orchestra, then Choir, before training at the Royal Northern College of Music. Now a professional soloist and voice-coach).*

Little did we think, as the family McDonald moved from "up North" to what we described as "down South", that we would very quickly make lifelong friends in Suffolk and join a musical group that would have such an impact on our lives. Mum and Dad joined the choir, and I still have a very special memory of Dad singing a solo part in Horovitz's Horrortorio, and Janet Dann orating dramatically, with such style and elegance.

I started on the back desk of the second violins and gradually, over many years, rose to the dizzy heights of front desk. I had been inspired by violinists such as Nigel Jay and Adrian Brown (who I later actually sang for when his conducting career took off) and I learned so much, especially in their sectionals and in full rehearsals with Dr. Chris Green's masterful leadership from the podium. My brother, Andrew, joined the brass section after a few years, playing trombone with his friend, Keith Doust, from the Salvation Army in Felixstowe. I can still remember whenever I tuned the orchestra, the gentle teasing from that brass section when I asked them to tune, and my Northern accent was very apparent in the way I pronounced that word!

Trianon has forged friendships, Jane Lloyd, clarinet, was at school with me, her brother Hugh was a fellow violinist and their father was in the wind section. Richard Reaville was a violinist who, as you may know, embarked on the same musical career move as myself and studied to become a singer. I know my decision to go the RNCM to train my voice surprised a few people, but Trianon was very supportive and helped me through the transition(!) by enabling me to perform as leader in my holidays and also sing some solos, especially when we went abroad. These trips opened new doors for me in many ways; travelling, meeting the Asef family and gaining confidence playing such pieces as the Bach double violin concerto, and singing various classical and light repertoire. I seem to remember performing in a building that must have been a convent, because before we all got on the coach to go back to our accommodation, I just had to run up the hill, imagining that I was Maria and singing as loud as I could, the theme song from the Sound of Music!

One of the many concerts at the Royal Hospital School especially sticks in my mind. We had just given a very spirited performance of Carmina Burana and as we left the hall at the end of the evening with the monks' words ringing in our ears, we walked out of the doors, through the pillars to be greeted with an almighty clash of thunder and blinding lightning forks slicing through the dark sky over the parade ground. It still gives me shivers and tonight's concert on 14th September will evoke so many memories.

I am so grateful for the musical education, opportunities and comradery I have been fortunate enough to experience with Trianon, and continue to do so. This is a very special weekend when we will enjoy making music together again, remember treasured memories and those no longer able to be with us in person, but I am sure will be in spirit. Let us join together as RVW has composed, "in sweet harmony", now and always.

**BEV RUDDOCK:** *Fifty plus years on*

*(Former member of the Orchestra, now long-term member of the Choir, Ipswich Arts Representative on Trianon's Committee, and Choir Librarian)*

My membership of Trianon now spans 50+ years, and it would take up far too much space to relate all my recollections and experiences here. Suffice it to say that as well as enjoying all the playing and singing – yes, all those years ago I started off in the percussion and violin sections of the orchestra, and sang as well – I have also been very involved on the administrative side. Currently I am a Trustee on the Management Committee as the group's Ipswich Arts Association Representative.

Down the years these jobs have, naturally, changed. Nothing's done in quite the same way now – thanks to modern technology, social media, etc. I didn't realise how much it really had all changed until I was recently asked to take on the job of Choir Librarian again. "Yes", I happily said, little realising how much more complicated it now seems – maybe it's just me getting older – but now that I've settled into the job again it's a bit like "water off a duck's back" and I have to admit, I am actually enjoying it!

January concerts sitting on the front row, enforced nowadays thanks to a RTA in 2009, it is always fascinating to watch the percussion section dodging around to play different instruments with such dexterity and determination! Trianon Tours are a particular favourite – I will always remember the one to Detmold, Germany, when a certain member of the brass section managed to miss the coach home. I'm sure others will have other memories, but we still always have such a good time, musically and socially. Bring on Warwickshire October 2019!

—§—

**LENIE VAN DER WAL:** *A view of Trianon from across the North Sea*

*(Secretary of partner choir, l'Espérance and, together with her husband Aart, a long-time friend of Trianon)*

"Lenie at l'Espérance 125th anniversary celebrations"

First of all, our warmest congratulations with Trianon's 60th Anniversary. A milestone, both from a choral and social perspective! Yes, l'Espérance is even (much) older, as our roots even go back to ancient times, to 1892, to be exact. But this is not a contest between two very special choral communities! On the contrary, we keep the most gorgeous memories deep in our hearts since we first met in 1997, and when we first sang together in 1998. It all comes down to our credo that singing together is much more than solely singing. Is there anything more beautiful and compelling than sharing and practising not only our love for choral singing, but also participating together in those many events, gatherings and friendships throughout these many years?

We most vividly remember and cherish the generous hospitality of Trianon's members, their endeavours to make us feel comfortable at (their) home, how we enjoyed those lavishly prepared cakes, puddings and sandwiches, the various friendships that came from it, but also the magnificent landscape of East Anglia, the Trianon jubilee concert in the Ipswich Corn Exchange, that shattering performance in Snape, but also our visits to those many villages and small towns with their picturesque churches, where music was rehearsed and finally performed. Quite intriguing also to see and hear our British friends easily finding their way in what must be their second nature: singing!

But we also cherish those many moments when Trianon was with us in Holland, visiting together places like Delfshaven (Church of the Pilgrim Fathers), the Silver City of Schoonhoven, the concerts in the Rotterdam Scottish Church and St. Laurens, and, of course, in our 'home town', the IJsseldijk Church in Krimpen aan den IJssel. Also unforgettable experiences!

A milestone: 60 years, but we are quite sure Trianon will not just muse about that rich history, but will look forward, keeping up the same good spirits as it has maintained over the years. The future looks bright and despite all of the current political turmoil there will definitely be no borders between Trianon and l'Espérance!

—§—

**MADDY RHODES:** *More Memories*

Finally – Christchurch Street has become the address with which I have the longest association. Many hours have been spent around the dining room table there, masterminding every minute detail of all Trianon events. What has occupied more time than anything else? Possibly 'What shall we wear?', which in itself just proves that you can't please all of the people all of the time. Just visit the TMG archive for the answers which we came up with. We first went into long black skirts for the visits to Detmold, and felt very sophisticated. One year it was so hot that most of the ladies did a "Sandie Shaw" and performed in bare feet.

—§—

# CHAPTER SIX

# THE MILLENNIUM

*Well, planes did not fall out of the sky as the clock struck Midnight and a new Millennium was ushered in – Trianon embarked on its fourth decade with an exciting array of programmes and visits to mainland Europe - its conductor would not fare so well with a change of job and many periods of hospitalisation.*

For Millennials, this may come as "news" to you. The year 2000 was heralded as an apocalyptic year which, on the stroke of midnight, would be marked by planes dropping out of the sky, "smart" apparatus would stop functioning and even pace-makers might be upset by the "millennium bug"- whatever that did not turn out to be. In fact, at midnight on the cusp of the end of 1999 and 2000 nothing happened - it was all a big anti-climax. However, little did I know that this decade would be life-changing for me.

So, where do we begin? Inevitably with the beginning of the 41st season. Trianon had celebrated its 40th anniversary in 1999 and, as often seems the case, planning after such a celebration felt almost an anti-climax. What better way to start a New Year than with a programme of film music? So in January 2000 this is precisely what we did. Later in the year we would present a Trianon version of the *Last Night of the Proms* at Snape Maltings which, at that time, was quite a commitment for a non-professional organisation. Not only did it require considerably more financial outlay than concerts in our normal venues, but also meant persuading an audience to travel twenty or more miles further to a concert. Not that people needed persuading, because Snape on a late summer's evening provides a lovely backcloth to a musical event.

The year ended with two slightly unusual commitments for some Trianon members. The first was a concert to celebrate the Tercentenary of the Unitarian Meeting House in the centre of Ipswich. This famous eighteenth century building once stood in grounds relatively unobscured by surrounding buildings. Now it is dwarfed by the Norman Foster-designed Willis Faber building, itself an iconic landmark of the twentieth century and featured on a United Kingdom postage stamp. The Unitarian Meeting House, on the other hand, has not been featured thus, but should have been with its fascinating exterior and equally intriguing interior accoutrements, including a spy-hole to establish whether visitors were friendly or intent on disturbing the religious meeting of so-called "dissenters".

Whilst not the easiest of buildings in which to stage one of our Community Concerts, there was a certain fascination for the members of the audience who sat in the box pews (that is, pews which had an entrance door which would be closed for the service) and where the pulpit towers above the performers - it enabled the preacher to deliver a message above the heads of those seated at ground floor level, while remaining in eye contact with those seated in the gallery.

So, from one Ipswich religious building to another and we ended the year with musicians from Trianon giving the Ipswich Town Concert in December. For readers not familiar with these events, I should explain that, in 2000, the Ipswich Town Lectures was a brand new series created by a team which I chaired within the Ipswich Arts Association. It was part of two significant Millennial innovations - the first was the creation of eight major Hangings depicting the history of Ipswich, and the second was the series of free lectures and events held at Museum Street Methodist Church in the centre of Ipswich, in which the focus would be on the town and the surrounding area. Little did we think at the time that the series would continue and expand with hundreds of people attending each year to hear a series of speakers on some fascinating topics including the link between Shakespeare and Ipswich, the demise of some major industrial and trading names based in Ipswich, and so on.

The relatively short fifty-minute lunchtime concert that ended the first year of the Ipswich Town lectures was significant in another way for the Group. We had participated in the first year of a new and what would become a significant feature of Ipswich cultural life. Some 15 years previously, Trianon had similarly taken part in the opening events that marked the restoration of the Ipswich Corn Exchange as a public venue.

At this point, I should say that my professional career was changing quite rapidly, without me really taking time to assess what that meant. For some time I had been tasked by the University, then Anglia Polytechnic University (a mouthful to recite when introductions were needed), with developing "outreach" in a small part of East Anglia. In the East of England, we had the Open University for whom I had taught since its inception in 1970. That organisation had been created to enable thousands of people who had never been to University, to study part-time and at their own pace obtain a degree and therefore improve their chances of employment. The OU (as we all knew it) had a rocky start, especially when Margaret Thatcher, then Secretary of State for Education, threatened its closure along with the newly created Essex University, on the grounds that the two institutions were filled with "left-wingers" and were a malign force in the stability of British life.

Memory dulls and when I meet university students now I often reminisce about the politics of the late 1960s and early 1970s when higher education was going through a turbulent time. By that time I had long graduated and probably was seen as part of the institutional problem that many students perceived existed.

I know that my early career as a lecturer in higher education was spiced by retrieving students from police custody after they had been arrested in Cambridge for barricading, in protest about the Vietnam War, the US Ambassador to the United Kingdom in a well-known riverside restaurant. Other experiences involved trying to find some office space in the first weeks at a London Polytechnic when the building had been occupied by students protesting about Margaret Thatcher's decision to withdraw free school milk, and then having to confirm over the phone to a London policeman, the identity of other students who had got arrested in protests in Red Lion Square outside the US Embassy.

Remember there were no mobile phones or social media then. Word of mouth was the principal way in which messages got passed on, assuming that students did not use public telephones. And how that word got passed on! I often think back and wonder whether there were some notional "revolutionary event league tables" amongst certain London Polytechnics, for it seems that trouble in one would be the prelude to even more trouble in another. The problems at the Polytechnic where I had been appointed a Lecturer in Psychology was prelude to the long sit-in by students at Hornsey College of Art (itself the subject of many articles and at least one book).

Personally, the closest I got to all of this was when I was Course Leader for the undergraduate degree in Psychology. My team was accused by students in a national newspaper of building psychology laboratories that would be used for experiments involving humans, and linked to deprivation studies of benefit to the military. The truth was far different - but leaving that aside – the students' claim was based on experiments undertaken in the USA, which have become legendary within psychology, where volunteers were assigned roles as jailors and inmates and then observed - rather like a mix between *Love Island, The Only Way is Essex* and *I'm a Celebrity*. The experiment had to be abandoned after a few days because the role-playing got too real.

I digress. By 2000 my University was anxious to extend higher education to a wider population. East Anglia had four Universities (five if one included the Open University) and aspirations were low. There were many pockets of East Anglia where it was known that youngsters were under-achieving but would never consider going away to University or College for further study either for financial or family reasons, or both. So, my task was to create a network of partner institutions that would be franchised with courses validated by the University, enabling local students to study locally.

My work had started in the mid-1990s and by 2000, Anglia Polytechnic University (APU) was in partnership with a growing number of local colleges. The first was in King's Lynn when the College of West Anglia decided that this was a good way forward, followed by West Suffolk College in Bury St Edmunds, and then Lowestoft College. Colchester Institute was already a major partner and would be followed by Essex colleges in Thurrock, Basildon and Benfleet, and others in Cambridge, Wisbech, Huntingdon, Stamford, Peterborough and Norwich.

By 2000 I was responsible for the largest network of partner institutions in England and thousands of students studying for a range of higher education awards, ranging from Higher National Certificates and Diplomas through to Masters level. This involved myself and my team travelling thousands of miles each year, meeting with College Principals, lecturers and students as well as managing, through a large team, the quality, examination and award processes.

With some judicious timetabling of the day job, I was still able to continue working with Trianon as well as the University Choir which had been formed in 1991 in Chelmsford (there was another choir at the University's Cambridge campus). Of course, during that time I depended, as I do now, on the team that forms the rock-bed of Trianon's existence. Without that team and Guest Conductors, I suspect things would have quickly unravelled.

The success of the Regional Partnership of which I was now Director brought with it other invitations and over the years before and after the Millennium I was invited to join various government-funded organisations responsible for Higher Education, including a major committee of the Higher Education Funding Council for England as well as another under the umbrella of the Quality Assurance Agency (the body responsible for monitoring the quality of work undertaken by Universities). Both provided me with a fascinating insight into the politics of higher education, but the acid test came with another appointment.

In the late 1990s I had been approached by a civil servant and asked if I was interested in developing an even wider partnership in the East of England that would contribute towards the Labour government's pledge to widen Higher Education. Tony Blair had made a commitment that 50% of 18-year-olds would enter higher education. I now know that target to be wide of the mark, but at the time it was like watching the emergence of Mount Everest out of a haze. Would we really be able to get anywhere near that?

Before a decision could be taken, I had to share the invitation with my boss, the Vice-Chancellor of the University, who made it abundantly clear that the University would release me only if I could combine it with my day job. After all the University paid my salary. At the time and with the urgency of civil servants behind the request, I agreed and so I became one of nine so-called "Strategic Leads" in England. My responsibility was to facilitate the expansion of Higher Education in the East of England. There were nine regions in the country, hence that number and my responsibility now extended beyond the four notional counties of East Anglia - Essex, Suffolk, Norfolk and Cambridgeshire - to include Bedfordshire and Hertfordshire.

So the scene was set for a number of years with me spending days back at base in Chelmsford, and others commuting to London or distant parts of the East of England - whether it was Peterborough, down to the Thames or Luton and Great Yarmouth. I can still remember the routes and stopping places. Everything was going swimmingly- or so I thought.

The seeds of change - looking back - were set when the then Vice-Chancellor announced that he was taking early retirement. I and other members of the management team met candidates for the post when they came for interview, and all of them responded with the "right" answers when it came to the almost unique nature of APU as a Regional University. Yes, they would support the enterprise and embrace the success that it brought. They acknowledged the national interest in this innovative approach to widening participation and the kudos it brought with it. For example, I and members of my team had been invited to appear before the House of Commons Select Committee for Higher Education, together with many invitations to speak at regional and national conferences.

The year of change was late 2003 when a new Vice-Chancellor was appointed and soon it became apparent that words expressed at interview and actions afterwards are very different things.

Trianon was pursuing its annual run of concerts with innovative programmes such as the January 2001 *Musical Magic* including a tribute to Freddie Mercury and Queen with John Langley's new arrangement for Trianon, *Queenian Rhapsody*; a concert in May shared with our partner choir from the Netherlands, l'Espérance, at St Margaret's Church, Ipswich; and a Snape Maltings concert in September when our new President, Sir Malcolm Arnold was in the audience. He was an unwell man but happily celebrating his 80th birthday. We performed his four *Scottish Dances*. I think he enjoyed the performance but, to be honest, his physical and mental health was fast deteriorating and communication was not easy.

As you read earlier, I had first encountered the music of Sir Malcolm when Trianon programmed his *Little Suite No 1*. It was popular with players - tuneful, bright with a tinge of jazz. Later, when I became Chair of the National Association of Youth Orchestras I encountered Malcolm who was the Association's President. So, I was in a good position to recommend to

Trianon Management members that he should be invited to become our new President.

A visit to the Royal Hospital School to perform in its Chapel had long been a prized occasion for myself and members of Trianon. It always was a nerve-wracking experience- especially for those who had never been in this wonderful Romanesque edifice of a Chapel dating from the 1920s. The reverberation period of getting on for 8-10 seconds meant a very special way of working the music, otherwise one heard it two or three times judging by the echo. The organ - one of the largest in East Anglia - only served to complement the experience as members could tell when they performed Saint-Saens's *Organ Symphony*. Our good friend, Peter Crompton, then Director of Music at the School, was once again at the console and chose a registration that would produce a very special effect. In that he was successful as the thundering chords were heard. It was a wonder we did not need a defibrillator on hand to revive some of the audience who were seated at ground level with the organ and its pipes behind them. "Armageddon" was how one member of the audience described it. "Wonderful" is how I would sum it up.

The choice for 2002 – preceded by a Study Day – was Elgar's *The Dream of Gerontius*. For me this was a very special work because it was a favourite of my late father. It was the second time we had performed it. Somehow the ambience of the Royal Hospital School Chapel once again weaved a spell in which this heart-searching work could be appreciated with the Angelic Voices reaching all parts of the Chapel from the heights of the organ loft. *"Praise to the holiest in the height"* had rarely sounded more spine-tingling, although I am sure the same would be said by any conductor who has had the privilege to conduct one of the greatest British choral works. Indeed, that is not really even a correct description because the partnership of soloists, choir and orchestra make it the equivalent of a Wagner opera as the tale unfolds of Gerontius on his death bed and the journey he is invited to take.

Buoyed up by the success of the performance we looked forward to many more at this location. As we entered 2003, I did not think that it would be the year in which I lost my father whose renewed presence in our family after 50 years of absence was a minor triumph of love over loss. Was it coincidental that we had chosen Gerontius 18 months earlier to perform, a work in which he had sung as a member of the Royal Choral Society for so many years?

That year started with a sparkling January concert in which we had tenor John Moorman. Now John - a tenor with a great voice - could get carried away. And he did, which meant that afterwards he and his partner were in no great hurry to exit the bar at the Ipswich Corn Exchange. Had he known as he was supping a pint that his car was now firmly locked up behind bars at a local car park, he would have ensured a speedy exit. As it was, he had to phone an emergency number in the depths of night to retrieve his vehicle in order for him to return to the north. Hospitality was provided overnight by Maddy Rhodes (although she believes it was 1998 not 2003). Good old John., who sadly passed away recently.

Another Day School and another visit to Snape marked 2003 and then a tour of Germany which we had visited many times. We chose a new location in the western part of Germany where we met some old friends and gave concerts for which we were joined by members of the Anglia Singers and L'Espérance. My abiding memory of one of these concerts was our associate conductor, Jean Shaw, frustrated that her instructions to visiting choir members were being ignored, turning to me with her voice loudly projecting "That's it! I give up!" as she pointed towards various females of the choir who had not listened to her instructions about stage etiquette. I think her words were not understood by our Dutch colleagues. The language got slightly bluer, only moderated by the fact that we were about to enter the church in which, in a few minutes' time, we would be performing.

*Trianon at the Movies* - by now you would think that this theme had become part of our musical DNA - re-emerged in 2004, and one of the first pieces we programmed was by Carl Davis - *Keystone Cops*. Little did I think then that this prolific composer of film scores and concert works would kindly agree to compose music for Trianon to celebrate its Diamond Jubilee.

Between January and the summer 2004 we welcomed a new partner group to England - Kayley Kolot - a lively group of Israeli singers. The link had come about through my work at the University where I had supervised a number of students - including some from Israel – for their PhDs. One of them, Raffi Lev, then a senior commander in the Israeli police, was a singer and so we welcomed the choir of which he was a member, together with their lively and highly demonstrative conductor to give some concerts. How pleasurable it was.

Their visit was not without its preliminary challenges - language was one of them, but so too was security. I had learnt that whilst Israelis felt safe in the United Kingdom, a group might be subject to security threats. To that end we had to liaise with the local police force who assured us that everything would be alright – and of course it was.  As they prepared to leave at the end of the visit, I asked some of the singers what had been most surprising for them. "Not having to open our handbags as we go into shops" came the quick answer. Their lives were dominated by ever-present bomb threats, so even Britain (by now used to potential IRA bomb scares or actual bomb incidents) was seen as a "safe" place.

For me, there was an important decision to make. That came in June 2004 when I decided that I could no longer continue working with the current

Vice-Chancellor of APU and would resign. Summer rehearsals proceeded as did a holiday, punctuated by phone calls from College Principals asking what was happening? The once-strong partnership was now under threat because the Vice-Chancellor wished to reshape it in a way that was not acceptable to its partners. I was asked if I would continue in my role until April 2005, but I knew that this was three months too long, and so eventually it was agreed that I should leave in December 2004.

Fortunately, music provided a welcome retreat from what was developing into a confrontational issue involving many actors. Grieg's Piano Concerto and *Carmina Burana,* performed at Snape in September 2004, provided a great distraction before a return to the politics of higher education (and believe me, those politics can be vicious - after all, many politicians come from that sector and return to it when they leave Parliament).

By January 2005, I felt like a "free" person. I had left the University, cleared my desk and - with the help of colleagues - exited with some sense of achievement and dignity as well as a great leaving party. How I should have listened to the professional advice I had been given in the lead up to this point. "Put some water between your job and the next thing you do!" I was told by a professional career advisor employed by the University to assist departing senior managers. Did I heed that? No, I did not (and some readers may say that this is typical of me - not listening to advice).

I was now working as hard as I could for the Quality Assurance Agency as an Auditor of Higher Education: that is, as part of a small team that goes into universities to evaluate the quality of courses and the student experience. This involved travelling to different universities for a few days of intensive meetings and evaluations, followed by a tight time-table to write up a report which went into the Public Domain, and was eagerly read by the University under scrutiny as well as potential recruits.

All was set for a new direction. Meanwhile, we had struck up a partnership in Trianon with distinguished writer and columnist Dr Ronald Blythe, who had written verse for us. Two concerts involved him and a poem written for Trianon, together with a new composing competition to coincide with the Choir's 40th anniversary. *Holy Mr Herbert* was the title of verse which proved a challenge to the contestants, but a winner emerged and it was this choral setting that was premiered in March and repeated in June 2005.

Work was continuing apace, but a day visit to speak at a Conference in London proved a turning point. Feeling ill during the Conference, I returned to Essex and, after a few days of feeling distinctly odd, visited my local and friendly GP. Within hours I was admitted to the Medical Emergency Unit at the local General Hospital and there I remained for nearly two weeks as they sorted out my problem – irregular heart rhythms. Despite some excellent

"*Associate conductor, and principal player of the percussion section, Tom Rumbold.*" *Photo Credit Geoff Rogers*

"Clockwise from top left: Guest conductor – Steve Rumsey, associate conductors – Martyn Shakespeare, Neville Reeder and Jean Shaw."

treatment, the remedial measures proved short-lived and, before long, it was back into hospital for a second time which meant that conducting was out of the question. But Trianon was in good hands, and Adrian Brown once again came to the rescue as had Barry Salmon, Jean Shaw, Neville Reeder, Steve Rumsey, Tom Rumbold, David Ruddock and Martyn Shakespeare in the previous years, and since.

This time, things were different. Another long-stay in the Cardiac ward resulted in some strange interventions and a trip to the Operating Theatre. Again, I was released from what seemed an eternity of injections and blood tests. By now, I had been told I could not drive and so I became reliant on good friends and family to act as chauffeurs to and from various rehearsals and events, which tested many friendships and also the patience of the members of various organisations with which I was connected - not least Trianon.

"It's unlikely you are going to conduct again for a while!" was the verdict of the friendly GP, himself a musician. That I found devastating, especially since I now did not have a job – I had had to relinquish any work with universities and  was not ready for the scrapheap. "Take things easy" is not a phrase I have ever been comfortable with, but when walking even a few yards had become a challenge, and sitting down to garden, or experiencing blackouts, then common sense dictated that standing in front of a choir and orchestra was not exactly sensible. But I did it - or at least, did it for part of concerts. Jeffery Babb, a good friend from way back and an experienced conductor of choirs and orchestras came visiting from his home in Lincolnshire to conduct the April 2006 concert, and others kindly took to the rostrum for community concerts during this time.

By 2007 I was ready to return and did so for *Twelve Musical Days* in January. We had had fun trying to programme this concert with each day of the verse featuring appropriate music. I cannot remember precisely, but *Lords a-leaping* and *Geese a-crowing* caused the biggest challenges and you can look at the Trianon archive to find the results of this musical exploration. A welcome return to St John's Church, Cauldwell Hall Road, in April with a themed programme with *Youth* as its focus was the prelude to a third hospital admission - so more guest conductors were needed, and there were real question marks as to whether I could continue in my role with Trianon. However, at the back of my mind was 2009 – the Golden Anniversary - and that I wanted to be part of.

Despite the most recent hospital stay, I shared conducting the January concert with long-suffering Steve Rumsey with whom I had shared many moments as arts producer for Essex Radio – the company which I had helped form in the 1970s and which now was a successful commercial radio station. Stephen, a fine horn player and conductor, was part of the arts team which produced a weekly programme. He and I collaborated on a programme that (once again) included music by Carl Davis, and also a new medley especially commissioned from Andrew Burke recalling many of the great songs and themes which had featured in James Bond movies.

September, and we were back in the Royal Hospital School with Duruflé's *Requiem* and before that Saint-Saens's Organ Symphony. Once again, the mighty organ would almost raise the roof, boosted by the massed strings as the glorious slow tune emerges. The audience could (if they listened carefully) hear it three times thanks to the resonance of the Chapel at Holbrook. A great concert and the prelude to more visits, but that was not to be. A change of Director of Music and Head Teacher together with a different approach to involvement (or not) with local communities spelled disaster for us and, despite a repeated attempt to rescind decisions taken on purely business grounds, Trianon has never been able to perform again at the Royal Hospital School.

When my mates and I formed a youth group way back in the 1950s, and then a small orchestra which took to the public stage in 1959, little did we know that 50 years later, we would celebrate that with an even larger orchestra and a choir 100 strong at times. But 2009 had arrived and Trianon's Golden Anniversary had as well. The year included a number of commissions with Ipswich-based composer Andrew Burke providing *A Fistful of Hits* and a new-found collaboration with London-based composer Matthew Curtis, an *Overture 50 Not Out!*.

During the year we were also able to bring together verse by a close friend of my family, Dr Joanna Clark, and Trianon member and composer, Charmaine Cooper who provided the music. *Golden thread* was performed at Community Concerts. The climax took place at the Ipswich Corn Exchange in September 2009, when former and present members came together with Trianon's President, John Rutter and representatives from Braintree Choral Society UK, Braintree Choral Society USA, Kayley-Kolot, L'Espérance and French partners, Crescendo, together with our German friends for a weekend of joy.

Of course, it could not be a Trianon event without some memorable aspects to it. I was delighted to meet my close friend from my schooldays, John Hart. If you remember, John had been a member of the youth group prior to 1959 and was really one of the three that gave Trianon its name (Tri = Three and Anon = Anonymous). John, an Ipswich boy, now lived with his wife Lorraine in the USA, and flew over to meet with his mother and join us that weekend. The Americans from Braintree, near Boston (members of the partner choir of Braintree Choral Society, Essex), as always, challenged us with their energy and zest for life. Vicky, my alto-singing School Superintendent friend from Boston really thought that the poultry farm we passed on the way to the

Sunday Reunion lunch had chickens which bore numbers, and that one of the tasks of overseas guests was to collect a number at the venue and return to the farm to find the chicken with that number. Its fate was obvious. It took quite a while into the reception before a blow on my body revealed her standing behind me and some choice words were exchanged.

Meanwhile the lunch continued with a rolling slide show of Trianon over the years past, and speeches, after which people mingled. Amongst the mingling was Madeleine Rhodes, a central figure in all of this and being the helpful person she was - and still is - she offered to take the newly-born baby belonging to a member for a brief tour round the estate, so its parents could mingle. When approached by Orchestra Leader, Steve Browne, to retrieve his baby, Maddy refused to hand the offspring over saying it belonged to someone else! She had got the wrong child; it was Steve and Julie's newly born daughter and was identified by the baby boots. Whoops! Maddy is now a youngster who will be a potential recruit to Trianon as long as she keeps out of Madeline Rhodes's clutches.

But the day was not over for there were games on the field! These kinds of pastimes had long featured in the Trianon repertoire and could involve country-dancing (Germany) monocycle displays (Christchurch Park, Ipswich) and more - about which I will not recount. For the Golden Anniversary, there was a new addition: welly-throwing. You know the kind of thing – see who can toss a welly the longest distance. One of the American "family" (Val Clark, who claims to be a member of the "Green clan" having ancestors bearing that name from Norfolk, UK) took up the challenge, threw it the greatest distance and managed to plant a welly footprint over the face of Trianon member, Ivan Gilson, who stood there transfixed as the object flew toward him. But then Ivan has always had a penchant for things blonde and American Val was.

So, it was a case of Auf Wiedersehen, A bientôt, See-Ya, and Auld Lang Syne, hoping that we would all meet again.

# TRIPS DOWN MEMORY LANE WITH FRIENDS

**MATTHEW CURTIS:** *Trianon from a composer's viewpoint*

*(Matthew has composed new works for Trianon to celebrate both its Golden and Diamond jubilees)*

It is well known that 2019 marks the Trianon Group's sixtieth birthday. It is quite something for such a group to reach such an anniversary at all, and I have no doubt that this is due in no small measure to the remarkable continuous involvement of Christopher Green. I myself am also sixty this year and it is quite a thought that, when I was but a new-born, Chris was already one of the driving forces behind the group.

Chris and I first crossed paths nearly 20 years ago when he got in touch with me having become aware of my work through the release of some of my earlier recordings. This has led to splendid performances of several of my concert works by Trianon, in addition to commissions for the Golden and Diamond Jubilee years, for which I have been extremely grateful. I wonder if it is generally realised just how important it is that groups like Trianon enthusiastically embrace works by composers like myself who are drawn to write what one might call more accessible repertoire, which is largely shunned by the mainstream. In this way, I believe, Trianon makes a significant contribution to music-making not just locally but nationally as well.

Here's to the next sixty years!

## CATHY JOHNSON

*(Trianon soprano and member of Trianon Music Committee)*

I've been involved with Trianon on and off for more years than I care to admit to! I am now a stalwart of the soprano section, but actually first joined Trianon as a timid violinist whilst I was still at school. I still remember the piece I played at my audition (probably one of the most terrifying experiences of my life), and joined in time for a Christmas concert that included *Raiders of the Lost Ark*. This was unlike any music I'd ever played in the school orchestra and really tested my playing. The next concert featured the piece of music I was studying for my music GCSE – that's handy I thought!

I've participated in more than a few memorable concerts – when we tackled the 1812 overture and almost blew up the Corn Exchange during rehearsal, the 'canons' were so loud. And then there were the concerts with the Chelmsford Ballet - inviting a ballerina for tea before the concert was thrilling!

Work commitments meant I had a long break from Trianon, however my sister Victoria took up my place in the violins and my Mum, Kath, joined the choir. After I had my children, I returned to Trianon but as a singer rather than violinist. I've really enjoyed the small ensemble singing at community concerts as well as tackling some of the major choral works. My youngest son is following the family tradition and is looking forward to joining the second violins, once he's done a bit more practice!

—§—

## NAOMI JAMES

*(Member of the Cello section and currently Trianon's Publicity Officer)*

Whilst at university I played in Lincoln Symphony Orchestra and then I joined Trianon in 2006 when I returned and needed some motivation to keep playing. For the last 12 years I have been sneaking in late, occasionally at the wrong location, and only once forgotten my bow. I do, however, enjoy playing in some of Suffolk's loveliest buildings.

I first started playing an instrument at Primary school through the Suffolk County Music scheme, although the choice was between a brass instrument or a clarinet. I first started with the cornet, via a trumpet then a tenor horn but it was not meant to be. When I went to secondary school we were asked what instruments we would like to play and if the school had one we could learn. I wanted to play the double bass, but quite wisely, my mother wasn't keen on manoeuvring this about, so I ended up with a cello and have been in love ever since.

In 2010 I first joined Trianon's Management Committee as Ipswich Arts Association Representative and then Programme Editor. In 2015 I decided to relinquish the roles to others. However, I was commandeered to join the committee again in 2017 but as Orchestra Representative and now along with many others I try and publicise all our wonderful events and I do love the committee's staple biscuit, the pink wafer!

I don't think that I would have continued to play my instrument if it were not for the patience and kindness of other players. I hope that this continues for future members.

—§—

**MADDY RHODES:** *Friends of Trianon*

I suppose it's true to say that the Friends of Trianon have been in existence for as long as the group itself, even if in the early days they had no official title. The first 'Friends' (supporters, sponsors and reliable transport providers, encouragers etc etc ) were undoubtedly our parents, a situation familiar no doubt to parents of every TMG generation. Among the first of course Chris's mother Muriel Green who must at times have thought her home had been subsumed into concert hall/ mastermind HQ. Other homes were opened up to provide venues for musical soirees and fund raising events. As time went by the official Friends of Trianon was launched and for at least 30 years the Friends subscriptions have sponsored the Easter Concerts. The numbers and names on the list come and go, and often the people behind the list get in touch. These are mostly former members who write fondly of their time with the group, and how that membership has launched them into further musical activity. Close contact with the Friends has diminished with the introduction of BACS payments of subs, and Trianon News going directly from the printers. Emails have replaced letters through the post, but it is lovely to hear from long-standing Friends – and many have been very loyal through the years.

*And the Tours*

Detmold – Krimpen an der Ijssel – Paris – Arras – Worcester – Warwickshire and hosting groups from Arras, Berlin, Krimpen and Tel Aviv.

Oh the fun of it all. The problem solving, the friendships, the 'lost in translation moments', the music, the transport, the drivers, the miles travelled, the sight-seeing, the exhaustion, the elation, the stories, the jokes, the hilarity, the laughter, the hysteria, the holding your breath moments. Above all the wonderful people we've met, the concerts, the parties, and at the end of every tour the inevitable question, 'Where are we going next?' I wouldn't have missed a moment.

*"Maddy Rhodes with friends from Kayley Kolot (Israel)."*

# CHAPTER SEVEN

# AFTER THE GOLDEN ANNIVERSARY

*The Golden Anniversary had been a great success, but one of the things I have long known is that, after one success, can come a surprise – and not always one that is pleasant.*

Trianon had reached the end of a decade and everything was in place for the January 2010 concert which would be another interesting programme of film music. One of the challenges that has regularly beset Trianon is the availability of a regular rehearsal venue. Long gone are the days when Trianon members would make their way to the slightly run-down Ipswich Scout Headquarters in Arcade Street. Now our administrator would produce a complex template of rehearsal venues in Ipswich that would accept and house either Trianon choir or orchestra, or both. For the winter 2009 into 2010 it was decided to try a new venue – Trinity Park, Nacton - the home of the Suffolk Show.

During the 50 years of Trianon's existence we had experienced the challenge of bad weather, but rarely had to cancel a rehearsal – although occasionally having to foreshorten one. Over this winter there had been a few wintry showers, but now – at Trinity Park – we were on the brink of a major concert in three days' time at the Ipswich Corn Exchange.

The rehearsal in this new venue was not a great success. Apart from needing to have a rehearsal that brought choir and orchestra together, the secondary object was to assess the viability of Trinity Park as a venue which would accommodate the combined resources of the group. Certainly space-wise the experiment worked, but acoustically, the venue was inappropriate. So, it was with some trepidation that I approached the Saturday morning dress rehearsal at the Ipswich Corn Exchange. However, we never got to that point because, on the day before, there was a large downfall of snow which placed the Saturday rehearsal, and possibly the concert, in jeopardy.

Trianon had set up a system whereby in the event of bad weather, phone calls would be made to a small group of Trianon members living in different parts of the region, so establishing what local conditions were like. The reports were not good - most were snowed-in, with local side roads treacherous and even main roads difficult to negotiate. Things began to look bleak and it became more and more likely that the rehearsal and concert would have to be cancelled. By the end of the day, a decision was taken and – for the first time in fifty years - Trianon was to cancel a concert.

From there on, the rest of the day was filled with calls to the local radio stations to put out messages informing the public of the cancellation and arrangements for getting refunds for tickets. It is a tribute to the organisers and Ipswich Borough Council staff that only two people turned up on the night - one of them a Trianon member!

So, here we were with a concert rehearsed and ready to go, but no slot for it. Apart from the financial hit which Trianon took from not being able to perform one of its most popular programmes, we had a concert in hand which would be rescheduled for January 2011.

There was little doubt that the cancellation was, at the time, a shock to the system – not least in deterring future audiences who might be less inclined to purchase tickets for a winter concert because of the possible threat of bad weather. So it came as a morale booster when a large audience came along in February to enjoy a programme performed by strings and singers from the group, to launch the 2010 series of Community Concerts at Felixstowe's Trinity Methodist Church. The group repeated the programme in May of 2010 in Debenham.

Now members of Trianon's Music Committee could start planning a programme for 2011 in the knowledge of having one programme in hand - the cancelled January 2010 programme was re-scheduled for twelve months later. Drawing from the number of films that used classical concert hall works as a basis for their film scores, *Trianon At The Movies* showed once again what a wealth of ideas can be brought to bear in this kind of programme, without over-dependence on current block-busters (which, of course, are also featured). John Langley was a long-term acquaintance of mine. A professional singer and orchestrator, John and his wife, Heidi, now live in London but he has supplied a number of arrangements of medleys for Trianon over the years. One of John's arrangements was premiered at this concert with *A Disney Treasury* bringing choir and orchestra together.

Programme in hand notwithstanding, the Group had an important engagement in February 2010. Trianon's French partner group, Crescendo was coming to Ipswich *en masse* to give a performance. I should explain: Crescendo is a performance arts group based in Arras, Picardie. Arras is Ipswich's economic partner (the town of Ipswich has never been keen on "twinning" as such), and long had an active Ipswich-Arras Association. Costume, song and dance play a vital part in the performance of Crescendo as do sound and lighting effects. Together they bring to their performances a vitality that can be infectious. The technical requirements of Crescendo did pose a challenge to Trianon, but Suffolk New College came to the rescue by making available the atrium of their new building and, although acoustically it was a challenge, the performance of Crescendo with a small contribution by Trianon was to be the basis for many future such events.

By now the yearly musical activity of Trianon had settled into a pattern which seemed to meet the expectations of members and enabled smaller ensembles within the group to explore different kinds of repertoire. So, for example, at different times the strings, woodwind or brass might form small performing ensembles, whilst small singing groups could try out contemporary classics or folk and classical works which are more intimate. Four concerts planned around different community groups and raising hundreds of pounds for each of them is the result, as is the opportunity to bring the brand of "Trianon" to new audiences. A brief survey of places visited in this series reveals repeated visits to Museum Street Methodist Church, Ipswich, Henley Community Centre, St John's Church, Needham Market and St Mary's, Capel St Mary. At least one visit to an Essex venue is included each year when possible, reflecting the significant proportion of Trianon members who travel north from Essex to Ipswich for Trianon rehearsals and performances.

*"Roger Hanes - BT engineer, yachtsman, Trianon archivist and oboist"*

Trianon has long been privileged by having amongst its membership, members with technological skills. One of the benefits for Trianon is that its home base has long been close to the BT Laboratories at Martlesham Heath. This has meant an annual supply of graduates coming to Suffolk to work there. Some of them are musicians, and many have joined the ranks of Trianon over the years. The annual supply may be a fraction of what it was in, say, the 1970s, but still they come.

One of those who joined Trianon was Dr Roger Hanes. Oboist, yachtsman, former Officer and now Trustee of Trianon, Roger has long been responsible for maintaining the Trianon archive. One of the fascinating pieces of Trianon archive is the digest of works performed by Trianon. This covers every known programme performed by Trianon since its formation in 1959.

It provides valuable help to Trianon's Music Committee members who regularly consult the listings to determine what works were combined with others in previous programmes, or when pieces were last performed.

I have not, as yet, established which works have been most regularly performed by Trianon and whether there is a pattern that shows certain favourites at certain periods in the Group's history. I seem to recall that, for a long while, Gustav Holst's setting of *Turn Back O Man* was a work that would often end a programme. I certainly know that one work that has featured frequently has been Carl Orff's *Carmina Burana*. The Group first performed this iconoclastic piece long before it became a firm favourite with choirs. The big challenge for others is to field an orchestra big enough to make the most of Orff's slabs of sound, although a version does exist for two pianos and percussion.

*Carmina Burana* has been performed by Trianon in many of its major venues, but in 2011 it was featured at Snape Maltings in a programme that also included Britten's *Young Person's Guide to the Orchestra* – a first timer for Trianon. And if this was not sufficient excitement in the year, a large contingent of Trianon and its partner Essex choir, the Anglia Singers travelled to the Netherlands in the autumn, although minus its Artistic Director who had once again fallen ill.

Returning from Netherlands and the warm hospitality of partner Dutch group, L'Espérance, it was back to more innovative planning for 2012 which would include two community concerts based around the theme of Charles Dickens and Friends (including Trianon members suitably attired), a themed January programme, *Trianon on The Sofa*, based on the idea of pieces that makes up for an evening of easy listening such as *Barwick Green* (theme tune for *The Archers)* and *Devil's Galop* (theme music for *Dick Barton, Special Agent*), whilst the September Ipswich *Trianon Last Night of the Proms* included a rarity, a newly orchestrated version of the *Ipswich New Town Hall Polka*, orchestrated by Andrew Burke. The work had been written to usher in the Victorian Town Hall when it was opened. The original work in piano version had been lodged in the archives of the Suffolk Record Office and now revealed how the great and the good were entertained.

*Lights, Camera, Action!* provided a "big sound" start to 2013. The season included a guest appearance of former Trianon member, Adrian Brown, as conductor of April's major concert, which included Dvorak's final symphony, *From the New World*. But if the year's programmes had trodden a familiar path, this could not be extended to September's family-themed concert which included Malcolm Williamson's *The Stone Wall*.

I had met the Australian, Williamson, many years previously when I interviewed him for a radio programme. His reputation as a "hell raiser" had brought the position he held as Master of the Queen's Music into disrepute and was well deserved, as was his reputation as a "difficult" person to interview. Monosyllabic answers seemed to be the order of this interview, but there was no denying that when he came to write music that involved children, his talent was obvious. *The Stone Wall* depicted the English and the Scots at loggerheads in centuries past. Children from St Margaret's School, Ipswich provided sufficient noise as the tribes confronted each other across the Ipswich Corn Exchange.

However, it was not just Williamson's work that provided an unusual twist to the programme, but three works that were receiving premieres of one kind or another. Matthew Curtis, now a firm favourite with Trianon players, provided one of these works with *A Festive Overture*. Not quite a premiere, rather a re-working of a previous version. We also had Andrew Burke's new collection of London-inspired pieces for choir and orchestra, *London Calling*. The third work was a belated birthday present to me, commissioned by Trianon for a significant birthday in 2012. Ben Parry, conductor of the National Youth Choir of Great Britain and son of my former music master at Northgate Grammar School, John Parry, had been asked by Trianon to write a work for Choir and orchestra for me. The result was *In Celebration of Music*, which received its first performance at the concert.

Three new works in one programme may not be a record for music groups, but it does underline the reputation that Trianon has acquired for supporting new music, although one of the disappointments is that many new choral works are written for smaller ensembles of singers who could rehearse the works over a longer period of time than is available to Trianon musicians.

With all this, it was a wonder that any further musical activity could be contemplated in 2013, but there were two more community concerts and a visit to Arras for four days. Once again, members of Trianon and the Anglia singers were able to share their music, laughter and plenty of community dancing with members of Crescendo. With Arras playing such a major role in the Great War, it was not surprising that a number of members (including myself) took the opportunity to visit the graves of family members buried in Commonwealth Cemeteries. One of the names of composers that was located was that of George Butterworth - a contemporary of Holst and Vaughan Williams - who had died in the Battle of the Somme. His name would be prominent in the commemorations that would occupy the thoughts of millions in the coming year.

The mention of George Butterworth reminds me that it was a chance encounter on a Saturday afternoon stroll through North London with one of my sons that led us to the English Folksong and Dance Society HQ. The building was open and we ventured into the library where I met the librarian. She showed me the latest digital mapping undertaken which indicated

*"John Moorman (tenor) performing with Trianon in A Night at the Opera at the Ipswich Corn Exchange (September 2010)." Photo credit Geoff Rogers*

*"The family factor - Ivan Gilson (centre) holding hands with Pat and Elaine Fisher, mother and wife of Trianon's Chair, during Auld Lang Syne at Chris Green's 70th birthday party (November 2012)." Photo credit Geoff Rogers*

"French partner group Crescendo's ebullient performance in Arras during Trianon's tour to Pas de Calais in 2013."

"Left: Chris Green with current President of Trianon, John Rutter CBE, leaving Suffolk One after a singing workshop led by John and (right) the workshop underway (2013)." Photo credit Geoff Rogers

where folksongs were collected. I had been giving a series of lectures about music in East Anglia and was fascinated with the frequency with which Essex and Norfolk songs were collected, but comparatively few from Suffolk. To my surprise, the librarian mentioned that George Butterworth had collected three folksongs from Ipswich! Now, folksongs and Ipswich do not easily go together, even though my grandparents would have associated Ipswich with living in a market town. Manuscripts of the songs for solo voice, of course, turned up. I mentioned it to a member of the Trianon Choir, Mim Macmahon. She, in turn, offered to arrange them for SATB. The result? A sixth work to add to our Diamond Jubilee offerings.

In 2014 Trianon, like many other organisations, had long been planning how members would mark the outbreak of the Great War. Discussions had been taking place during many meetings of the Music Committee and gradually a set of guiding principles had emerged. Members knew that the programme should not be celebratory or contain music that might be associated with any particular country. Of course, there were certain composers whose names were linked with the Great War especially Butterworth and Ralph Vaughan Williams.

The programme that emerged turned out to be one of Trianon's most creative, starting with poetry by A.E. Housman read by Trianon's own "narrator-in-residence", Janet Dann, followed by George Butterworth's orchestral work, *A Shropshire Lad*, based upon the same verse. John Williams's haunting music for *Warhorse* followed, with Vaughan Williams's *Towards an unknown region* concluding the first part of a programme that had been accompanied by a rolling Roll of Honour as names of family members killed during the Great War were screened.

Long before any other East Anglian group had performed Karl Jenkins's *The Armed Man*, it had been performed by Trianon, and members returned to it for the second part of the programme, *Peace and War*. Rarely had a work evoked such a strong emotional response from both audience and performers alike which could be almost felt as the closing chorale of *The Armed Man* came to a hushed conclusion with *God shall wipe away all tears*.

After the intensity and evocative images of the Great War, it required a very different kind of programming to launch 2015. That January programme had more than a passing reference to the Great War with a selection of songs arranged for choir and orchestra by Stephen Hogger. *Tommies' Tunes* drew upon many of the songs popular amongst the service personnel in the Great War and used in Richard Attenborough's film adaptation of Joan Littlewood's *Oh, what a lovely war!*

Guest Conductor, Stephen Rumsey, made a welcome return visit to conduct the April 2015 concert which was followed by the first visit from a choir from Saxony. St Johannis Chorale was based in a town south of Berlin. The link had been forged many years earlier through a very indirect route. The Pastor of the church at which the choir was based was the daughter of a friend of mine, Hildegard Pörtner, who had visited England in the 1960s as one of two interpreters with the youth orchestra from Detmold. She married and had two children, one of whom, Stephanie, would enter the Lutheran Church. Herself a keen singer and organist, Stephanie had been instrumental in arranging concerts for Trianon, the Anglia Singers and L'Espérance when they had visited Germany a few years previously.

Blessed with some excellent jazz musicians, the German group joined with Trianon for concerts in Ipswich, and then it was not many months before Trianon and its partners were off again to Arras for concerts in the historic Town Hall, where health and safety restrictions seemed to be a thing of the future, as well as giving a lunchtime concert in the Student Building of the Arras campus of the University of Picardie.

*On the Bright Side!* certainly lit up January 2016 especially with Eric Idle's song *Always Look On the Bright Side* and Arthur Wilkinson's clever adaptation of Beatles' songs recast as movements from Tchaikovsky's *The Nutcracker Suite. The Beatlecracker Suite* had a chequered history emerging as a series of "fillers" written for TV transmissions of *Sunday Night at The Palladium*. However, performed together the suite made up a happy feature of the programme and reminded me that it is a great shame that Trianon cannot perform a similar work by its President, John Rutter. John's *Beatles Concerto* managed to hit No 1 in the charts, but for copyright reasons, the work is not available for public performance,

Snape Maltings is the right kind of venue for Walton's *Belshazzar's Feast*, for it not only allows one to maximise the size of the choir but also the orchestra with its two additional brass bands required for the celebratory part of the work which made such an impact at the Leeds Triennial Festival in the 1930s. For the second time, Trianon programmed this complex work with its double choirs and semi-chorus plus sequences of irregular rhythms. Now, I have to admit that Walton is one of my favourite composers – there is such a vibrancy to his music, and that admiration was further underlined by the many times I sat in the Leeds Town Hall where the work was premiered and where I was a student. I also met a number of singers who had sung in the original performance under the direction of Dr Malcolm Sargent who had been assigned the unenviable task of conducting the premiere when the Conductor of the Leeds Triennial Festival – Sir Thomas Beecham – decided that he had to be elsewhere.

When at Snape, one is always aware of Britten's presence, especially in the Green Room – the backstage space assigned to the conductor. I have long

*"Guest Conductor, Stephen Rumsey, performing with Trianon at St. John's Church, Cauldwell Hall Road, Ipswich (April 2015)." Photo credit Geoff Rogers*

*"Trianon Community concert at the Unitarian Meeting House, Ipswich (October 2018)." Photo credit  Fred Ixer.*

sat, waiting for the cue to go on stage, looking at Britten's portrait that hangs in the Green Room. On this occasion I wonder what he would have made of Walton's music being performed in "his" building, for the two were hardly the best of friends and, if musical legend is anything to go by, the relationship became even more strained after Walton's one-act opera, *The Bear*, was performed at the Aldeburgh Festival containing (as it did) a jibe in the direction of Britten's partner, Peter Pears.

Occasionally, the Group has been faced with the dilemma of changing a programme to address certain national or international events that have taken place within the short time before a concert. 9/11 forced many Americans to remain in the United Kingdom until flights to the USA resumed. Some found their way to Snape and a programme that had been changed slightly to address this cataclysmic event. The same thing happened following the death of Princess Diana, but there was one event which created unintentional consequences for us, looking back. Not for the first time, the Music Committee had chosen a programme for September 2017 that had brought together British and American music under the programme title of *Across the Pond*. Little did members of the Committee imagine that the American Presidential Election and the arrival of Donald Trump might have a knock-on consequence at the Box Office. In the event, attendance at the concert was lower than usual despite an attractive programme. Feed-back later on revealed that, even at this stage, the idea of listening to American music at the time of post-Election was proving one step too far. No wonder that the subject of Brexit has never once emerged during current programming,

After the shock of the emergence of President Trump and the consequences for the arts, it was a relief to find new audiences when Trianon embarked on the first autumn musical tour within the United Kingdom. Quite how the change of policy came about is not certain, but maybe there was justification in exploring Britain's countryside after repeated visits to Germany, the Netherlands and Northern France.

After taking soundings amongst the membership of the group, various options were considered and eventually Worcester was identified as the centre for a four-day visit that proved one of the best undertaken by Trianon. Careful planning by Trianon's team ensured a variety of different experiences including a fascinating visit to Belmont Abbey, near Hereford, coinciding with a programme being screened the same evening on BBC 4 about the Abbey. A talk by the Abbot and a chance to meet many of the Brothers including my own nephew was a privilege, as was a chance to perform the final concert of the tour in the church where Elgar's father and Edward himself were organists, St George's Roman Catholic Church. These concerts were only a few of the highlights of the tour which included visits by many of the musicians to local drop-in centres and care homes as well as forging a link with a local Methodist church which hosted rehearsals by the Group who, in return, gave a lunch-time concert and then joined in Sunday morning service.

Trianon marked the onset of the Great War in 2014 and, at the time, it was resolved to mark the end of the War in 2018 but not before the Group brought a slightly quirky interpretation of *The Twelve Days of Christmas* in January 2018. After all, the concert coincided with Twelfth Night but the challenge of choosing suitable music for each day of celebration proved an exercise in lateral thinking with ideas abounding but few workable.

Before Trianon returned to Snape in September, the usual community concerts were duly delivered at Alresford in Essex and Henley, near Ipswich. The former venue enabled us to view the new extension to this community church designed by my eldest son, professional architect and Trianon's Concert Manager, Jonathan Green. For the latter concert, Trianon teamed up with a Suffolk-based charity, Music in Our Bones, which organises music groups supporting those suffering from Alzheimers and Dementia. Whilst Trianon strings and singers provided the bulk of the programme, it was inspiring to welcome members of MiOB to contribute musically and to raise one of the largest collections to support their work.

As a result of the experience, Trianon's Management team resolved to adopt a proposal made earlier in the year by Be Bird, former Chair of Trianon's Music Committee and a member of the music team, that one charity should be chosen for the entire Diamond Jubilee Year scheduled for 2019. So it was that Music in Our Bones was chosen and, as a sad postscript, Be died unexpectedly in the summer of 2018, shortly after the death of her husband, Richard.

Trianon has experienced the loss of many dear members during its 60 years. In some cases, their departure was after serious and long-term illness. In the case of Be, her death was entirely unexpected and, therefore, came as a shock to so many of our members. She had been a vital source of energy in the Group for a long time, conducting rehearsals, along with Jean Shaw and Martyn Shakespeare, serving on the Music Committee as its Chair, and singing in the alto section. She conducted her own choir based at the Ipswich Institute; all of this was combined with a demanding set of family responsibilities. It was fitting that in 2019 we should promote, along with her musicians from the Birkbeck Singers and St Andrew's Church, Rushmere, a memorial concert.

So we reach 2019 and Trianon's Diamond Jubilee: three major concerts, three community-based concerts, workshops, various initiatives including crowd-funding for no less than six commissions to be performed during the year which ends with the second UK tour, this time to the Coventry area.

—§—

*"Be Bird sitting with Elgar during Trianon's trip to Worcester in 2017."*

# TRIPS DOWN MEMORY LANE WITH FRIENDS

**STEVE BROWNE**

*(Violinist and pianist, member of Trianon's Music Committee and the longest-serving Trianon Orchestra Leader)*

When I did the research to remind myself when I took over as Leader of Trianon Music Group, whilst I knew it has been a long time, even I was surprised to learn that it has been 22 years, making me the longest serving Leader of the Group.

People often ask me, "what is it like to be the Leader of an orchestra"?

Well, the answer can be described in many different ways: a responsibility, exciting, nervy at times, a privilege. You are very proud when things go well, a little frustrated when they do not.

The role has many different responsibilities. You quickly realise that if you don't play in the right place at the right time, very often the entire section will not follow you. By being a strong player, you encourage and hopefully inspire others. You work out how things should be played. You certainly help the conductor to achieve what he or she is looking for and sometimes suggest different ways of doing things. And there is a role to play, particularly in our Group, of encouraging younger players to learn the art of orchestral playing and build their confidence. As indeed it was for me.

But with Trianon, it does I think go further. You are actually part of that big family helping the very well-oiled machined to function. A particular commitment is the Music Committee, which I joined immediately on taking over, and have served ever since, helping to shape our varied repertoire, encourage audiences and eating many, many biscuits.

I have many fond memories, too many to list and have made many long-lasting friends. Joining the Group helped to catapult me into the music scene in Ipswich and beyond, having moved to Ipswich in 1993 to work for the then Guardian Royal Exchange, now AXA.

I sincerely hope the Group will continue for many years.

--§--

## SIMON FISHER: *My Life in Trianon*

*(Member of the Bass section of the choir, longest-serving Chairperson of Trianon. Four members of his family (including Simon) have been or are members of the Group)*

I joined Trianon in 1982 whilst doing my A-levels. I had sung and also played violin for many years at school, but when I went off to study electrical engineering at Liverpool University, sadly my violin days came to an end. I continued to sing with Trianon when I returned from University in the holidays, and even when I eventually went out to work in London for 3 years, before returning to Suffolk to work at BT Research at Martlesham.

Very soon I was spotted by the Trianon 'talent scouts' and offered the opportunity to be the Group's Publicity Officer. For the next four years I was responsible for producing and distributing leaflets, posters, fliers and programmes, as well as capturing sponsorship.

The next step in my Trianon career was to be Treasurer. This proved a real eye opener, as managing all the income and expenditure exposed me to the multitude of activities that go on to allow Trianon to deliver its concerts and book music and venues up to two years into the future. It also allowed me to develop a good understanding of charity rules and regulations. Being still fairly young and naive I completely failed to spot that the 'talent scouts' now viewed my knowledge of finances and charity law, plus an inability to ever say no, as ideal credentials to be Chairman. And so in 2005 it came to pass that I was elected Chairman of the Group, and have continued in that role right up to today.

Over that time, I must say that it has been an absolute pleasure and an honour to be part of the management team that has organised all the concerts, tours, bursaries, community events, competitions and celebrations. Trianon is a truly great organisation that provides musicians of all abilities the opportunity to develop their musical skills and knowledge, and perform in both large and small concerts. Furthermore, the Group has helped raise many thousands of pounds for other deserving charities and organisations. Here's to many more great years of performing!

--§--

# CHAPTER EIGHT

# ENCORE!

So reader, I have been grateful for your company in this journey of sixty years, and I hope you have enjoyed some of our adventures and meeting some of the people who have contributed to what Trianon has become, and is, in 2019. We have come to the last chapter in this current story-line, and I trust it will not be the final chapter in Trianon's history.

When planning concerts, I and the team which makes up Trianon's Music Committee, always find it difficult choosing the work that is going to conclude the programme. It has to be up-tempo? Or does it? It certainly needs to involve both choir and orchestra in most cases, and one would like to think that it has the audience on its collective feet – but it is some time since I ever saw that happen in Suffolk. The best answer one usually gets to the question "How did you think the concert went?" is "Yes, it went ok!". Now in Suffolk parlance that usually means it went "well", but to the outsider it is a significant downplay of the end result.

By now you will have worked out that Trianon was an "accident" waiting to happen. It was never intended to continue past the point that its founders finally grew into adulthood and went off and earned an honest income. That it did continue suggests that there was a spark there and it needed to be kindled. My job (along with many others) has been to keep the spark alive.

There have been many challenges during the sixty years, but maybe we are facing some of the most significant ones to have arisen for some time - for example, the decline in school music is regretted nationally, and rightly so. When Trianon was formed, many schools had thriving instrumental ensembles or even school orchestras, and choirs. Many children were able to benefit from instrumental tuition at an affordable rate at school. Now, much of this has been dismantled and only the independent school sector can maintain extensive musical activities. Whilst I applaud that, I have to say that the engagement of such schools with local communities can be fragile.

When Trianon was formed, it provided a route through secondary years into further and higher education, with many students continuing their music on leaving school and maintaining membership of Trianon. For some, that route was to be career-changing and they sought to make music their occupation, helped in more recent years with a ring-fenced bursary fund available from Trianon.

Trianon has always had a somewhat hand-to-mouth existence where rehearsal halls are concerned. This stems from the fact that the pattern of rehearsals does not sit easily with those who hire out venues. Obviously hirers need a regular income to maintain the existence of their halls and a weekly booking is always to be favoured over the seasonal bookings that make up a Trianon rehearsal schedule. We have rehearsed in great barns of buildings, in former sports centres, in cold redundant churches, and occasionally we have come across a warm, well-lit and spacious hall with acoustics that are helpful to either choir or orchestra. Sometimes, and increasingly we are being gazumped by commercial organisations that can pay above the odds for premises and so the continuing challenge is to maintain a portfolio of rehearsal venues.

In the early days, Trianon members made great use of medium size school halls and other premises for their concert. Audiences grew as did both choir and orchestra and we outgrew many of these venues. In the 1970s, we were fortunate to be able to start using the refurbished Ipswich Corn Exchange, and how good it was to be able to transfer our forces from unsuitable educational premises into a hall that possessed an acoustic that was helpful to performers, and had an organ (installed, by the way, by volunteers prior to the re-opening of the Corn Exchange). Alright, the backstage facilities are cramped, and we cannot get all the performers on stage, so the orchestra has to be positioned at ground floor level, but it provides a sympathetic environment in which to perform, and is double the size of the largest of our other venues with the exception of Snape Maltings.

From its inception, Trianon has always needed to fill as many seats as possible, not only because the economics of promoting concerts demands it, but also because it is good to play to a "full house". We have been able to do this through maintaining Trianon ticket prices at an affordable level, and providing attractive, fresh programming.

Looking through the programme archive, I am continually amazed at some of the little-known works that we have performed during our existence. How many non-professional choirs have performed Liszt's *Missa Choralis* or Carl Orff's *Carmina Burana* long before it became the hit of the late twentieth century? But the music publishing industry has changed in the lifetime of Trianon almost beyond recognition. Gone are the myriad publishing houses, with many of the smaller companies swallowed up by a few big players, many of whom have transferred their main office from the United Kingdom to other countries.

Public libraries often had extensive music and drama sections from which one could borrow orchestral and choral sets at a modest fee, and which would regularly add stock. Many of the major music libraries have closed and their assets scattered. In short, choosing a programme that is fresh and innovative has never been a greater challenge. Yet we have managed to do this and attract audiences with regular commissions, and our record shows that we have given first performances of works at the rate of nearly one in every year of our sixty years.

Of course, there is the other elephant in the room - the inevitable ageing process, and judging by the longevity of many conductors, that is something which gives some sense of optimism. To be more realistic, as long as the downbeat can be distinguished from any other arm gesture, then there is hope!

Trianon has, in contemporary parlance, become a "brand", but I hope that what it says on the tin is what one gets. I like to think of it as a family, but then maybe that is an over-romantic view of what the organisation is like. On the other hand, I have known many acts of great kindness and times when there has been a strong sense of loss in our collective musical life, and however one might complain at times about the feeling of "Here we go again!", would we have it any other way? I cannot answer for you. All I can say is that I would not.

Looking back over sixty years, I have a strong sense of pride in the friendships that have grown. In some cases, they have resulted in longer-term partnerships. But whatever the state of being is, Trianon has survived and from the original three, the family of musicians has grown.

"Trianon on the steps of Ipswich Town Hall, c.1975"

"Trianon at Snape Maltings Concert Hall 2018"

# APPENDIX

## PRESIDENTS

| | |
|---|---|
| Imogen Holst | 1961 - 1984 |
| Peter Aston | 1985 - 1995 |
| Malcolm Arnold | 1996 - 2006 |
| John Rutter | 2007 - Present |

## CHAIRS

| | |
|---|---|
| Roy Coates | 1959 - 1970 |
| Eric Ogles | 1970 - 1975 |
| Frank Dames | 1975 - 1978 |
| Eric Hague | 1978 - 1980 |
| Alan Shotton | 1980 - 1984 |
| Ivan Gilson | 1984 - 1993 |
| Janet Dann | 1993 - 1997 |
| Neville Reeder | 1997 - 2000 |
| Alan Wilcox | 2000 - 2005 |
| Simon Fisher | 2005 - Present |

## LEADERS

| | |
|---|---|
| 1960 | Carol Long |
| 1961-64  part 1965 | David Lewis |
| 1965 | Irene Underwood |
| 1966 | David Lewis |
| April 1966 | Nicholas Foster |
| September 1966-1967 | Howard Griffiths |

| | |
|---|---|
| 1968 | Nicholas Foster |
| April 1968 | Carolyn Baldwin /Graham Wells |
| Summer 1968- 1970 | Adrian Brown |
| 1971-1972 | Jane Footit |
| April 1973 | Nigel Jay |
| September 1973 | Elizabeth Dixon |
| 1974 | Elizabeth Dixon / Alison Francis |
| 1975-1977 | James Chapman |
| 1977 | Margaret McDonald /Jayne Lodge |
| 1978-1979 | Margaret McDonald/Paula Radford |
| 1979 | Paula Radford |
| April 1980 | Paula Radford /Annette Clarke |
| 1981 | Annette Clarke /Peter Bumstead |
| 1982 | Annette Bumstead née Clarke |
| 1983-1986 | Elizabeth Hawes (Beaton from 1985) |
| 1987 | Alan Humphries |
| 1988-1989 | Elizabeth Beaton |
| 1990 | Elizabeth Beaton /Alan Humphries |
| 1991 | Elizabeth Beaton / Isobel Reaville |
| 1992-1996 | Isobel Reaville (Goodier from 1994) |
| 1997 – Present | Steve Browne |

## PREMIERES AND FIRST PERFORMANCES

Premieres (*) denotes Trianon's commission of a work and its first performance. A "First Performance" may not be a commission.

| | | |
|---|---|---|
| Appleton, Michael | The Silent Cortege | 1972 |
| Barrell, Bernard | A Holiday Overture | 1964 |
| Barrell, Joyce | Concertino for solo | 1964 |
| Barrell, Joyce | A Child is born in Bethlehem | 1980 |
| *Boulter, Ian | A Tribute to Disney | 1991 |
| * Brown, James | A Miniature Symphony | 1965 |
| Brown, James | Divertimento | 1967 |
| Brown, James | Fantasia | 1968 |
| Bumstead, Peter | Sinfonia Concertante | 1981 |
| Bumstead, Peter | Variations for string quartet | 1978 |
| * Burke, Andrew | A Fistful of Hits - Golden Year | 2009 |
| * Burke, Andrew (arr.) | James Bond Medley | 2012 |
| * Burke, Andrew | Couch Potato Suite | 2007 |
| * Burke, Andrew | London Calling | 2013 |
| * Burke, Andrew (arr.) | A Tribute to Rodgers and Hammerstein | 1995 |
| * Burke, Andrew (arr.) | Some more Rodgers and Hammerstein | 2015 |
| * Burke, Andrew (arr.) | The Musicals of MGM | 2013 |
| * Burke, Andrew | A Cluster of Diamonds | 2019 |
| Butterworth, arr. Mim MacMahon | | |
| | Three Folksongs from Ipswich | 2019 |
| * Cooper, Charmaine | Golden Thread | 2009 |
| *Corp, Ronald | Jubilant Song! | 2019 |
| Curtis, Matthew | A Diamond Overture | 2019 |
| Curtis, Matthew | A Festival Overture (revised version) | 2013 |
| * Curtis, Matthew | Overture: 50 Not Out | 2009 |
| Dann, Lewis (arr.) | Eighteenth Century Dance Suite | 1981 |
| * Davis, Carl | Jubilee Fanfares | 2019 |
| Enfield, Patrick | Christmas Eve | 1968 |
| Godball, arr Burke | Ipswich New Town Hall Polka | 2012 |
| Green, Christopher | A Short Fanfare | 1964 |
| Green, Christopher | Scenes | 1961 |
| Grimwood, Anita | Holy Mr Herbert | 2014 |
| * Hawes, Jack | Choral Suite | 1966 |
| Hawes, Jack | Christ is born | 1971 |
| * Hawes, Jack | Piano Concerto | 1971 |
| * Hawes, Jack | Pieces of Eight | 1998 |
| Hawes, Jack | Prelude- In Celebration | 1974 |
| * Hawes, Jack | Seven plus Two | 1974 |
| * Hawes, Jack | The Bells of Youth | 1966 |
| * Hawes, Jack | Three English Lyrics | 1966 |
| Haydn, transcribed Green | A Harpsichord Suite | 1962 |